Networks for Faith Formation

Networks for Faith Formation

Relational Bonds and the Spiritual Growth of Youth

STEVEN EMERY-WRIGHT
and ED MACKENZIE

WIPF & STOCK · Eugene, Oregon

NETWORKS FOR FAITH FORMATION
Relational Bonds and the Spiritual Growth of Youth

Wipf & Stock
An Imprint of Wipf and Stock Publishers
199 W. 8th Ave., Suite 3
Eugene, OR 97401

www.wipfandstock.com

PAPERBACK ISBN: 978-1-4982-3602-7
HARDCOVER ISBN: 978-1-4982-3604-1
EBOOK ISBN: 978-1-4982-3603-4

Manufactured in the U.S.A.   APRIL 25, 2017

To Lorraine,
the partner who,
filled with the patience of Job,
encourages my faith development.
—S. E.-W.

To Ali,
bone of my bones,
flesh of my flesh,
beloved partner in Christ.
—E. M.

Contents

List of Illustrations and Tables

Preface

WHILE THE CHURCH'S MISSION is for people of every age and culture, our conviction is that there is a particular need to nurture the faith of young people, especially in North America and Europe. As numerous studies have shown, the failure of the church to retain its youth is the primary reason for its decline, and there is a real need for those who bear the name of Christ to seek wisdom in this area.

While there are many helpful guides to help with such a task, our argument in this book is that adolescents need a range of networks for faith formation, relational bonds that help faith grow. While the importance of such networks is not limited to young people, they are particularly crucial during adolescence as young people explore issues of identity, purpose, and faith.

In the pages ahead, we describe eight networks for faith formation, drawing on biblical studies, practical theology, and the social sciences. We seek to show how each network can significantly shape a young person's faith, and offer ideas for those wishing to embed such networks in their own context, whether as church leaders, youth workers, or parents.

Our collaboration in this book represents a shared passion for faith formation, and particularly the formation of the young. We are grateful for all who have formed our faith, and thankful to God, who has called us as "citizens with the saints and also members of the household of God" (Eph 2:19).

Steve Emery-Wright
Ed Mackenzie

Acknowledgments

THANK YOU TO FRIENDS who have supported us in this project, including members of our church families who have modeled faith to us, demonstrating in word and action God's ever-active grace.

Thanks particularly to those who have entered into conversation and debate over faith and young people. Your thoughts have sharpened our own! Thanks to colleagues and students at Cliff College Derbyshire and Trinity Theological College Singapore, as well as friends at the International Association for the Study of Youth Ministry.

Thanks to our families, who shape in our homes networks of faith formation that continually support and sustain us! Thanks especially to our wives, Lorraine (Emery-Wright) and Ali (Mackenzie), who both read numerous versions of the book, put up with late nights in our studies, and offered constant support. Thank you!

Having collaborated on the book, we are grateful for each other's graces and gifts and the opportunity to work together on a project close to our hearts.

Introduction

Why Networks for Faith Formation?

It is ... when teens' family, school, friends, and sports lives and religious congregations somehow connect, intersect, and overlap that teens exhibit the most committed and integral religious and spiritual lives.

CHRISTIAN SMITH AND MELINDA DENTON[1]

A STORY OF NETWORKS

GROWING UP IN A Christian home, Jill had learned a lot about God.[2] She learned that God had created the world, sent his Son, and given his Spirit at Pentecost. She learned too that the Bible has sixty-six books and that God somehow spoke through it. Her parents also modeled faith in the home, reading the Bible with her each week and teaching her how to pray. Her gran would also talk with her about God whenever she visited.

It was when Jill became a teenager that she really felt faith had become real. Her church had employed a youth worker for the first time ever,

1. Smith and Denton, *Soul Searching*, 162.

2. While this story is fictional—or at least a composite account of stories we have encountered—many of the stories in *Networks for Faith Formation* are of real people and real churches. In all cases, we have changed their names to protect anonymity.

and—joining the youth group on Friday night—Jill found space where she could ponder faith and pray with her friends, as well as enjoying the games they played together. Jill also attended the youth rallies in the nearest city, and meeting with young people from all over the county helped her faith grow.

By the time she left school, Jill had built a network of relationships connected to her faith. As she looked back, she could see how strongly such networks had shaped her. Without them, it was hard to imagine that her faith would have survived.

Ryan had also been part of Jill's church, but, unlike Jill, had not come from a Christian home, and grew up knowing little about Jesus. When a Christian friend invited him to the youth group, Ryan thought he would give it a try, and liked it enough to keep coming back, week after week. After a year or so, Ryan expressed a dramatic conversion at a youth rally. He felt a sense of his own sin and God's love and forgiveness as he committed his life to Jesus, and as he returned home he experienced a surge of enthusiasm for praying and reading the Bible. An enthusiastic Christian, Ryan continued to be a part of the youth group, meeting up with Christian friends and the youth pastor every Friday evening.

When he was sixteen, Ryan's family moved to a smaller town, and he began to drift in his faith. His friends tried to stay in touch, but their lives were busy and he slowly lost contact with them. He tried the local church but it seemed old and stuffy. Ryan managed to just hold on to his faith, but found it difficult to pray or speak about Jesus. When he started college, Ryan embraced a hedonistic lifestyle, deciding that the Christian group on campus was not for him. His faith lay behind him, shed off like an old coat. It was fine while it lasted, he thought, but life moves on.

It is likely that you have met a Jill or a Ryan, and perhaps their story echoes part of your own. While many Christians come from a Christian background, some also enter the church through conversion. Most Christians also come to faith during their teens, and this was true of Jill and Ryan.[3] Where their stories differ, however, is in the support that each received throughout their youth.

Jill's story reflects the importance of networks for young people, networks that crisscross age brackets and sustain faith while it begins and

---

3. While Jill grew up in a Christian home, it was as a teenager that she felt she embraced the faith for herself.

grows. Like Jill, all Christians need relationships to help them grow as disciples, and this is particularly important during adolescence.

Ryan's faith, while apparently genuine and heartfelt, was difficult to sustain without the support of others, especially in an environment that was indifferent to his faith. Without such relationships, it is likely that faith will wither and die, like a branch separated from a vine or like a seed sown on concrete.[4] There is always hope for people like Ryan, but how much better to provide the necessary networks of support for the Ryans of this world at the earliest stages of their faith? How much better than risking another prodigal?[5]

NETWORKS FOR FAITH FORMATION

"Networks for faith formation" is our description of the range of relationships that help to nurture and develop faith. They are the relational bonds through which God works to build up the church.[6] They are the connections, events, and occasions that help us to discover more deeply the God who calls us and saves us.

The importance of networks does not mean that an individual believer *cannot* come to faith without them, nor should it imply that all such networks are of equal value. God graciously draws people to himself through various means, and a person from an atheistic background who comes to faith in their late fifties is as valuable to God as the person born and nurtured within a Christian family. The values of the kingdom undermine any sense that those born into a set of networks have any superiority over those who come to faith from outside the church.[7]

4. This is not to privilege relationships to others over a relationship to Christ, since relating to Christ also takes place within the context of other relationships. See chapter 1 for further development of this theme.

5. The failure of churches to retrain their youth is a well-recognized problem across North America and Western Europe. For a 2007 survey of the dropout of youth from church, see McConnell, "LifeWay Research." For a British account of why Christians walk away from their faith, and thoughts on how to respond, see Frost, *Losing Faith*.

6. The term "relational bonds" is used in various fields, but in our use refers to a strong relationship between an individual and another person or group of people. For a similar use in practical theology, see Root, *Relational Youth Ministry*, 199–207.

7. Many Christians, however, fall into the opposite temptation of privileging the experience of those who come to faith from a non-Christian or anti-Christian background, particularly if it has been characterized by wild living! While such conversions are to be celebrated, the salvation of anyone, whether or not they are born within a Christian

Our contention, however, is that the Scriptures, theology, and sociological studies reveal the importance of a range of networks for growing faith. God has created us as relational beings, and this means that spiritual growth requires relational bonds and social connections. Such connections represent channels through which Christians can love one another, and it is such love that should characterize those who follow Christ (John 13:34–35; Rom 12:8; 1 John 4:7–8). The thicker the web of relationships, the more likely it is that faith in Christ will grow.

FAITH FORMATION AND YOUNG PEOPLE

While networks are necessary for growing in holiness at every stage of life, they are *particularly* important for young people, those between eleven and twenty years of age.[8] During adolescence, teenagers undergo massive physical, emotional, and intellectual changes while also exploring issues of identity and purpose.[9] At the same time, teenagers are given little power or responsibility and are typically segregated from the adult world, much to their detriment.[10] As emerging adulthood becomes a more distinctive life-stage, the age of responsibility and maturity recedes further and further into the future.[11]

At such a life stage, young people desperately need a range of healthy and God-centered relationships. Recognizing the importance of networks for faith formation means that church leaders, youth workers, and parents think strategically and intentionally about how to identify, create, and sustain such networks for the youth that they serve.

The significance of networks for the faith formation of young people is good news for the church! Friendships, adult interactions, and even encountering people from different backgrounds take on new and key significance in shaping a young person's life.

family or raised in the church, is a gift that leads even the angels to celebrate (Luke 15:7).

8. While many approaches to youth ministry focus on thirteen- to eighteen-year-olds, there is an increasing recognition that adolescence is beginning earlier, while adopting the upper age of twenty highlights the need for churches to ensure networks of faith formation are in place for those transitioning to work or further education.

9. For a description of developments during adolescence, see Jacober, *Adolescent Journey*, 49–73.

10. On this point, see Allen and Ross, *Intergenerational Christian Formation*, 35–46; and DeVries, *Family-Based Youth Ministry*, 35–57.

11. On Emerging Adulthood, see Smith and Snell, *Souls in Transition*, 4–17.

Such a focus can complement other resources on the Christian formation of youth, such as those focusing on spiritual practices,[12] mentoring, [13]
or vocation.[14] It can also complement those works offering a broader theology of spiritual formation among young people.[15]

The importance of attending to a broader ecology of relationships
or networks is also found in other works.[16] Dean and Foster, for example,
helpfully identify the importance of relationships for young people, and
show how youth need a range of different kinds of relationships to flourish
in their faith, including with parents, mentors, and friends.[17] *Sticky Faith*,
a work that aims to equip parents to build lasting faith in their children,
points to the importance of helping kids develop relationship with other
adult figures within the church, as well as with Christian peers.[18] While the
theme of *Intergenerational Christian Formation* is obvious from the title, a
key emphasis throughout the work is that of helping young people (and all
within the church) build relationships with Christians of other ages.[19]

As well as works in youth ministry and practical theology, sociologists
also point to the importance of multiple networks in building faith. Mark
Regnerus's study of teenage sexual activity and faith, for example, found
that belief and commitment to God were insufficient for helping young
people follow their faith's teachings on sexuality. What was needed was a
range of networks to support young people seeking to live their faith. Such
networks including parents, key adult figures, a supportive faith group, and
close friendships.[20]

While *Networks for Faith Formation* draws from the wisdom of
other practical theologians and social scientists, it seeks to offer a more

12. See, for example, Oestreicher and Warner, *Imaginative Prayer for Youth Ministry*;
and Jones, *Sacred Way*.

13. See Mayo, *Thriving Youth Groups*.

14. White, *Practicing Discernment with Youth*.

15. See Heflin, *Youth Pastor*.

16. As well as the following works, see the discussion of how important a "sense of
belonging" is for teenagers who stay in church in Lytch, *Choosing Church*, 24–44. See also
the study of Thompson, who found that emerging adults who stayed connected to church
in the Presbyterian Church of Ireland had relationships *both* with a peer group *and* with
a wider church family ("Keeping Close to Home," 212).

17. Dean and Foster, *Godbearing Life*.

18. Powell and Clark, *Sticky Faith*.

19. Allen and Ross, *Intergenerational Christian Formation*.

20. Regnerus, *Forbidden Fruit*, 196–98, 203–7. See also Stroope, "Social Networks."

structured treatment of eight key networks, so giving a broader view of the way in which faith is formed. It takes an interdisciplinary approach, drawing on biblical studies, practical theology, and the social sciences, while offering practical guidance for how those within the church can strengthen networks for faith formation. While the argument that networks are essential for faith to grow applies across cultures, our focus will be on North America and Europe, the contexts we know best.

Our hope is that *Networks for Faith Formation* can empower church leaders, youth workers, and parents to evaluate their own practices of faith formation for young people and for the church. Our final chapter offers tools that leaders and parents can use to help them in this task.

WHAT ABOUT THE SPIRIT?

While our argument draws on the social sciences, as well as Scripture, a stress on networks for faith formation should not be seen as in any way undermining the role of the Spirit. Networks are about relationships, and it is through relationships that the Spirit changes us. It is typically in community that we grow. Spiritual gifts are given, as Paul notes, "for building up the body of Christ, until all of us come to the unity of the faith and of the knowledge of the Son of God, to maturity, to the measure of the full stature of Christ" (Eph 4:12–13).

As the Bible reveals, followers of Christ from the very beginning have always existed within crisscrossing networks of relationships. Such networks nurture faith and connect it to a surrounding culture. It is through such networks that the Spirit works.

In the New Testament, the gospel invitations to follow Christ always involve a summons to join other followers of Jesus.[21] The dramatic conversions to the way of Jesus, such as the woman of Samaria (John 4:1–42), Zacchaeus (Luke 19:1–10), and Levi (Luke 5:27–32), impacted the group of disciples as well as the rest of the community. The Pauline injunction to "live your life in a manner worthy of Christ" (Phil 1:27) only becomes possible within the church as the body of Christ. And the risen Jesus of

21. Jesus' instructions to some of his converts to stay where they are, or return to their communities (Luke 8:38–39), may seem like exceptions to the rule. In each case, however, the expectation is that the new disciples will spread the word about Jesus within that new community, and so create a new group of disciples within each locale. Jesus' post-resurrection call to make disciples explicitly calls for initiation into the church through baptism and instruction (Matt 28:18–20).

Revelation addresses the *churches* of Asia Minor, rather than primarily its individual members (Rev 2–3).

Contemporary theology has also emphasized community through its appeal to the Trinity as the divine community that makes sense of human relationships and ultimately gives them their rationale and purpose.[22] The network of Trinitarian relationships, as it were, grounds the networks of human relationships found within the world.

It is not surprising, then, that accounts of spiritual growth within the Christian tradition typically include a communal dimension. Whether we speak of means of grace or spiritual disciplines, such practices include a focus on relationships and networks that involve other people as well as God. God works through such networks to shape all, whether young or old, to become like Christ.

OVERVIEW

Networks for Faith Formation begins with a discussion of the theology of relationships (chapter 1) that grounds the need for networks that nurture Christian faith. Such a theology draws on the biblical portrayal of God as relational as well as its description of humans as created for relationship. The sociological observations that also shape our work rest on the theological significance of networks.

In chapter 2, we discuss the importance of personal faith practices ("bedroom practices"), since these are where churches, parents, and youth workers often start when thinking about spiritual formation. Such practices are necessary for a life of faith, and are ways in which God's grace is manifested within the lives of individuals. They also, however, require other networks of relationships that provide the broader context for an individual's faith to flourish.

Chapter 3 sketches the importance of the church as the key network within God's economy of grace, and contends that regular participation in worship shapes believers. Sociological evidence for the importance of church life in Christian formation supports the biblical emphasis on the church as the community where the Spirit dwells and where the use of gifts and graces leads to growth into the image of Christ.

In chapter 4, we turn to the importance of the family. Scripture, of course, highlights the role of parents in sharing the mighty acts of God and

22. For a description of this development, see chapter 1.

passing on the faith. Research supports this scriptural theme and shows how parental faith and involvement has a huge impact on young people.

The role of friends is the focus of chapter 5, and the importance of such relationships for faith—picking up a scriptural theme—is a theme of recent research on faith development. For young Christians in particular, having a group of peers who share their faith can help them sustain it in an often hostile environment.

Chapter 6 explores mentoring relationships. While friends relate as equals, a mentoring relationship is typically one in which a mature Christian models faith to a younger person, supporting and encouraging them. Mentoring relationships are found within the Bible and a range of recent works recognize their growing importance today.

In chapter 7, we focus on the role of small groups for the faith formation of young people. Recent years have seen a resurgent interest in the role of the small group in faith settings, and such groups can claim a strong historical pedigree. Such groups also help young people keep the faith in a social context that is often hostile or indifferent to it.

For children and young people, attending a pilgrimage, camp, or festival can have a huge impact, and the significance of such events and gatherings are discussed in chapter 8. While they have some drawbacks, events and gatherings are particularly helpful in situating faith within a larger Christian context and helping young people see the vibrancy of faith.

In chapter 9, we explore the importance of mission and service in developing the faith of children and young people. Whether in local communities or further afield, mission can lead to transformation. While mission trips have been criticized by some, they also have potential to strengthen and encourage young people in their journey of faith.

Chapter 10 will offer some ideas for adopting a networks approach to the faith formation of young people. The chapter offers a simple tool for evaluating such networks in the lives of young people, as well as some ideas for encouraging a process of deep theological reflection. As we shall argue, such an approach invites every member of the church to look out for the young in their midst. If you are particularly interested in practical application and want to see how this approach might work in your church, you may want to start with this chapter!

In the appendix, we offer some brief reflections on the role of the online world, and particular social media, in helping or hindering the faith of young people. As networks of communication, social media tools are widely used by young people today, and so need to be addressed in any approach to spiritual formation. Rather than giving a prescriptive list of dos and don'ts, we offer instead five broad principles for such engagement and signpost useful resources in this area.

Our aim throughout *Networks for Faith Formation* is to explore such networks in a way that is biblically based, sociologically grounded, and contextually relevant. As we do so, we hope to provide insights and tools for all who are interested in nurturing the faith of young people and others within the church.

1

Grace through Networks
A Theology of Relationships

Every detail involved in love and worship requires personal relationship with others, with family and friends and neighbours—responding, receiving, giving—and with Father, Son and Holy Spirit—also responding, receiving, giving.

Eugene H. Peterson[1]

INTRODUCTION

What is it that makes someone holy? How is it that some people find themselves transformed and shaped by God in a more visible way than others? What causes the change?

There is no simple answer to this. God shapes us in a number of different ways, and only a holistic account of discipleship can do justice to the way the Spirit works. What does seem to be the case, however, is that relationships and networks are necessary for spiritual growth to take place.

Personal spiritual practices alone, for instance, are unlikely to shape young people to be like Christ. While such practices are necessary for growing in faith, they need to be embedded within other relationships, including participation in church. As we shall argue in chapter 2, without such relationships, spiritual practices are likely to weaken or become connected to a faith that loses its center in the triune God of grace.

1. Peterson, *Practise Resurrection*, 220.

While the church is crucially important, attending worship alone is also insufficient for spiritual growth. As Wesley recognized, there are many "almost Christians" within churches, those who go through the motions of faith without being transformed by the Spirit.[2] If taking part in worship were the key factor for shaping lives, then we would expect the United States of America, with nearly 40 percent church attendance,[3] to be one of the holiest countries in the world. We would also be surprised to find that Nigeria, with nearly 90 percent attendance in worship each week, suffers high levels of corruption.[4] If we embrace a narrow understanding of how God works to bring about spiritual growth then we end up with the illusion of spirituality and the delusion of growth.

In this chapter, we will focus on three key biblical and theological themes that point to the significance of networks of relationships for spiritual growth. First, God is a God of relationship, a theme reflected in God's self-revelation as Trinity and God's covenantal engagement with his creation. We are, second, created for relationship, as the creation account particularly attests. Third, we are shaped through relationships, and so the Bible emphasizes the need for connection within the community of faith. Each of these claims provides a theological framework for the understanding of relationships and networks that we will explore throughout this book.[5]

As well as drawing on Scripture, we will show how contemporary theology and research in the social sciences supports the idea that relationships are fundamental to our identity. These sources show how growing in a life of faith for young people (and, indeed, for people at every stage of life) requires a set of formal and informal relationships, networks for faith formation through which God's grace flows.

---

2. For Wesley's classic sermon on this theme, "The Almost Christian," see Wesley, "Sermon 2."

3. Newport, "Frequent Church Attendance."

4. According to Transparency International, Nigeria scores just twenty-seven out of one hundred on the "2013 Corruption Perception Index" (Transparency International, "Nigeria's Corruption Challenge").

5. For a different approach to the theology of relationships, see Root, *Relational Youth Ministry*, which, drawing on Bonhoeffer, explores relationships as the site of God's presence.

THE RELATIONAL GOD

For many young people today, God is a distant, grandfatherly figure looking at the world from afar but scarcely interested in it and certainly not concerned about the interior lives of its inhabitants. As Christian Smith notes, for the majority of American teenagers, "God does not need to be particularly involved in one's life except when God is needed to resolve a problem."[6] Studies of youth spirituality within Britain have also shown how God has tended to be pushed out of the self-understanding of young people. Even when young people believe in God, their spiritualty tends to be this-worldly and imminent.[7]

In contrast to such a view, the God of Scripture is personal and relational, the Lord of creation who stakes a claim over all that he has made. God created the world but also constantly sustains it.[8] The Spirit who nurtured creation continues to oversee it with care, while not even the death of a sparrow escapes the notice of the heavenly Father (Matt 10:29).

The relational nature of God is reflected particularly in the biblical depiction of God as a covenant-making God. Covenants within the biblical world were binding commitments between two parties. Unlike contracts, covenants were relational agreements, and involved both sides committing to an ongoing relationship, with all the benefits and obligations that implied.[9] Throughout the Bible, it is through covenants that God primarily relates to his human creation.

The Old Testament points to a range of covenants between God and humanity, each of which show God graciously entering into relationship with his people.[10] In the covenant with Noah, God promised to avoid flooding the world again (Gen 9:1–17), while the covenant with Abraham involved God's promise that Abraham's descendants would be a "blessing

6. Smith and Denton, *Soul Searching*, 164. Smith and Denton use the term "deistic" to describe this part of teenage religiosity, but see also their fuller description of "Moralistic Therapeutic Deism" (ibid., 119-71).

7. See Collins-Mayo et al., *Faith of Generation Y*, esp. 83–89.

8. In his study of the Old Testament, Fretheim notes that God exists in "genuine relationship with every aspect of creation and intimately involved with every creature" (*God and World*, 20). Fretheim makes the point about the Old Testament, but such a theme is also found in the New.

9. Routledge, *Old Testament theology*, 163.

10. For an overview of such covenants, see Dumbrell, *Covenant and Creation*; Gentry and Wellum, *God's Kingdom*; Hafemann, "Covenant Relationship," in Hafemann and House, eds., *Central Themes*, 20–65; Routledge, *Old Testament Theology*, 159–74.

to the nations" (Gen 12:1–3). The Mosaic covenant (Exod 19–24) followed God's redemption of his people from Israel, and included covenant stipulations for God's people. In the Davidic Covenant (2 Sam 7:12–13), God also promised to raise up a descendent of David as ruler of the nations.

The Old Testament also points forward to a new covenant (Jer 33:31–34; Ezek 36:24–28), when God empowers his people to keep the law. The law will be written "on their hearts" (Jer 33:33), and God will give them a "heart of flesh" (Ezek 36:26). The new covenant also brings a greater knowledge of God's presence; God will be known to his people, and they shall know God (Jer 33:34). As God proclaims through the prophet Ezekiel, "you shall be my people, and I will be your God" (Ezek 36:28).

The claim of the New Testament, of course, is that Jesus is the mediator of the new covenant (Heb 12:24 cf. 2 Cor 3:6). In Jesus, as Paul writes, all God's promises are fulfilled (2 Cor 1:20). Jesus sees his death as establishing this new covenant (Luke 22:20), and in this new covenant God reconciles networks of Jew and Gentile, man and woman, free and slave (Gal 3:28).

Astoundingly, Jesus is not simply a messenger of the covenant God, but is himself the presence of the covenant-making God. Jesus, "the Word who was with God," became the incarnate Son of God (John 1:1–7). Jesus is the image of God through whom we see God's character and in whom we are drawn into God's presence (Col 1:15–20). Jesus is the Son of God who reveals God's covenant of grace with the world. As Karl Barth puts it, Jesus Christ "is the maintaining and accomplishing and fulfilling of the divine covenant as executed by God Himself."[11]

While the biblical covenants show how God relates to humanity, the doctrine of the Trinity, the God who is three-in-one, shows most explicitly the relational being of God.[12] While the full-fledged doctrine developed over the first few centuries of the church, its roots are found in the New Testament (Rom 1; Matt 28; John 1).[13] The church's teaching that God is "one God in three persons" seeks to do justice to the biblical teaching that there is only one God alongside the scriptural view that Father, Son, and Spirit all share in the attributes of the one God.

The Trinity points to the relationship between the Father, Son, and Spirit. God is a relational God because the Father, Son, and Spirit have

11. Barth, *Church Dogmatics*, 34.

12. On this point, see especially Grenz, *Theology for the Community of God*, 68–107.

13. For New Testament inclusion of Christ in the "divine identity," see Bauckham, *God Crucified*.

always and will always exist in triune unity. While the relationship between the persons is a mystery we can only understand by analogy,[14] such a revelation of God's nature suggests that relationality is at the heart of the universe.

The Scriptures also attest that God draws us *into relationship* as Father, Son, and Holy Spirit.[15] As Paul shows in Romans 8, God the Father draws us by the Spirit into union with Jesus, the Son. We pray to the Father through the Spirit—sometimes with groans that words cannot express—and so share in the "sonship" of Jesus (Rom 8:15–17). A similar point is made in Jesus' High-Priestly Prayer, where Jesus asks that those who believe in him might be drawn into union with the Father (John 15:20–23). The purpose of the incarnation is to draw us into relationship with God. Here, the themes of covenant and Trinity come together; God wills to draw us into relationship, to "lift us up into a life of communion, of participation in the very triune life of God."[16]

While the relational nature of God is not something to which the social sciences themselves can attest, they do show that the hunger and thirst for transcendence remains a part of the human condition. For adolescents, the search for transcendence can be identified in the search for intense and ecstatic experience, getting high through drugs or other means.[17] It can also be traced in the near ubiquity of prayer among people of all cultures, even those who claim no religious faith.

A theology of networks, then, begins with the acknowledgement that God is relational. If God seeks to relate to the world as its creator and Lord, then seeking to relate to God is the foundation of a life rightly lived. Jesus introduces us into this relationship, but not without the networks we have with those around us.

---

14. Horton, *Christian Faith*, 299–301.

15. For a classical treatment of this theme, originally written in the seventeenth century, that is alive to the pastoral and practical implications of the Trinity, see Owen, *Communion with the Triune God*.

16. Torrance, *Worship, Community*, 21.

17. Dean, *Practicing Passion*, 93–115.

CREATED FOR RELATIONSHIP

As well as depicting God as relational, the Bible depicts humans as created for relationship. As the opening chapters of Genesis show, humans are made for relationship with God as well as for relationship with each other.[18]

The relational openness of humans to God is reflected throughout the creation narrative.[19] While God's creation of humanity in the "image of God" partly refers to the rule and dominion that humans exercise on behalf of God (Gen 1:28–30),[20] it also includes a relational dimension.[21] Only by knowing God can humans properly carry out his commissioning, and reflecting God before the world means relating to God faithfully.[22] As Routledge notes, "Human beings are made by God and for God and may find their full meaning only in relationship with him."[23]

God's engagement with humans throughout the Genesis narrative is a further indication of the human need to relate to God. God speaks with Adam and Eve, blessing them and commissioning them to look after his creation (Gen 1:28–29). The divine address to humanity requires a human response; a relationship is formed. God grants Adam and Eve freedom to eat of the garden, while warning them of the consequences of eating the "tree of the knowledge of good and evil." The "no" of God—the boundaries that exist—shows that this is a true relationship. God is no cosmic servant, but a covenant-making God who entrusts humanity with responsibility while always pouring out grace. The anthropological image of God who

18. A third form of relationality is relationship to the *land*. This is an important area, though cannot be considered here. For a helpful discussion of the land from a missional perspective, see Wright, *Mission of God*, 397–420.

19. As Cortez claims, "personal relationship lies at the heart of the creation narratives" (*Theological Anthropology*, 35).

20. For this functional understanding of the image of God, see Middleton, *Liberating Image*.

21. For a helpful description of different understandings of the *Imago Dei* ("image of God")—"structural," "functional," "relational," and "multifaceted"—see Cortez, *Theological Anthropology*, 13–40. Cortez also offers an approach to the image of God that seeks to embed a "relational" component within a "functional" interpretation.

22. While the term "covenant" is missing in Genesis 1–3, a number of interpreters argue that God's creation and commissioning of Adam and Eve can be understood as a covenantal act; so Hafemann, "Covenant Relationship," in Hafemann and House, eds., *Central Themes*, 40–42.

23. Routledge, *Old Testament Theology*, 140.

walks in the garden with Adam and Eve points to God's desire to be with those he has created (Gen 3:8).

Genesis 1–3 also points to the need for relating to others as central for the human condition. In Genesis 1, it is as "male and female" that humans are created in the image of God (1:27), while in Genesis 2, the relation of male and female is vividly expressed in the creation of woman from the rib of man (2:21–23).[24] The creation of Eve occurs because "it is not good that the man should be alone" (1:18). While the focus here is on marriage, the importance of human sociality is also implicit within this text. The marriage relationship is a kind of primary relationship that shows that being with others is fundamental to human existence.

God also commissions Adam and Eve to "go forth and multiply" (1:28), laying the foundations for the high value given to children in the Jewish and, later, Christian world. Children are a blessing from God, a gift that God gives to his people. Children remember the promises and deeds of the covenant-making God and pass them on to the new creation. Children grow through relating to their parents, and parents likewise grow through their responsibility for those they conceive.

The relationality within creation is not just an insight of Christian theology but is part of the human condition. "People are by nature social animals," Aristotle once observed, and forms of community are found in all human societies. As the psychologist Susan Fiske explains, we are indeed social animals at the core of our being. Our inborn nature, and the way we are nurtured, allows us to interact in such a way that we thrive both as individuals and as a community.[25] Through such interconnectedness, we build self-esteem and a desire for self-improvement. Trust is also nurtured in relationships, with healthy trust making us more adaptable, open to new experiences, and cooperative with others.[26] Arguably, it also makes us more open to respond to God.

Neurologists point out that our brain is hardwired for relationships. Relationships literally shape our brain and stimulate its growth. We are, so to speak, biologically hardwired for interacting with others, and are thus endowed with a "social brain."[27] This allows us to engage in complex social

24. For the implications of Genesis 1–2 for teenage sexuality, see Emery-Wright, *Understanding Teenage Sexuality*, 109–24.

25. Fiske, *Social Beings*, xx.

26. Ibid., xxi.

27. Vrticka, "Evolution of the 'Social Brain.'"

interactions and maintain multiple relationships. Our brains are further wired in such a way that we experience reward during mutual social interactions, and feel sensations similar to physical pain when we are socially rejected or disapproved. We have been perfectly hardwired for thriving in a world that is becoming ever more socially complex.

The scientific emphasis on the importance of relationships echoes a strong biblical theme: we are created for others, and we find life not in isolation but in relating to those around us.

FORMED THROUGH RELATIONSHIP

Since God is relational, and we are created as relational beings, it makes sense that we are formed and transformed in and through relationships. While many Christians talk of their transforming relationship with God, there can often be less of a sense of how other Christians transform us in and through their contact with us. This is partly due to the individualism that affects large parts of Western Christianity. Such individualism can tend to focus on "Jesus and me" to the exclusion of others, and naively assume that faith is a private journey rather than a journey that is always social in nature.[28]

In contrast to such individualism, the Bible emphasizes the importance of community. While this fits more comfortably within the Semitic context of the Scriptures,[29] it also reflects the need for Christians to prioritize relationships. In the New Testament image of the church, for example, to be "in Christ" involves relationships with others. The image of the body of Christ, and Paul's development of it in Romans 14 and 1 Corinthians 12, shows that members of the church need one another in order to grow fully into Christ.[30] There is no solitary Christian; we are all "one in Christ" (Gal 3:28). Only in community can we be formed to live for God.[31]

---

28. "Therapeutic individualism," which sees the self as the source of true knowledge, has a particularly pernicious effect on the spiritual formation of young people. For a description, see Smith and Denton, *Soul Searching*, 173.

29. The group focus of the New Testament is a particularly theme in Hellerman, *When the Church Was a Family*.

30. In chapter 3, we will explore in more detail the significance of the church as a primary network in Christian formation.

31. For the importance of Christian community for shaping disciples, see also Walton, *Disciples Together*, 28–40.

The Bible also speaks explicitly of the way in which the company of others shapes us, warning against associating with the ungodly and extolling the virtues of good company. The Psalms begin with a blessing on those who "do not follow the advice of the wicked or take the path that sinners tread" (Ps 1:1–2), while Psalm 133 extolls the relationships between brothers as one of God's good gifts. Proverbs 24:1 warns against envying the wicked, while Proverbs 2:20 encourages the wise to "walk in the way of the good, and keep to the paths of the just." Paul tersely expresses the point with his quotation of an ancient Greek proverb, "Bad company ruins good morals" (1 Cor 15:33), while also encouraging believers to love one another and agree together (2 Cor 13:11).

The way in which relationships shape us, for good or for bad, is also demonstrated in sociological studies. In one American study, *Hardwired to Connect*, the authors show that children and young people need nurturing relationships. Their claim is that it is precisely the absence of such relationships that lead to mental illness, behavioral problems, and emotional distress.[32] Without caring relationship, we are far more likely to lead lives that are dysfunctional in some way. When relationships with children and youth go wrong, there is an increase in the likelihood of depression and antisocial behavior. In other words, the presence or absence of a nurturing environment during childhood not only shapes a child's psychological and emotional development but also alters brain development in ways that profoundly affect long-term health. The authors of the study also claim that humans are biologically primed to seek moral and spiritual meaning, and nurturing relationships are central for this.[33]

Scripture and sociology remind us to be aware of the way in which our relationships shape us. The danger of being formed by those who lead us away from God, however, needs to be balanced with the example of those parts of Scripture that call followers of God to also meet and bless those outside God's household. Jesus associated with sinners and tax collectors, inviting them into his kingdom. And while Paul warns against associating with Christians who persistently sin, he recognizes that Christians should not seek to break off relationships with all the ungodly—or they would need to leave the world!

32. Commission on Children at Risk, *Hardwired to Connect.*

33. For an overview of research that shows the difficulties that teenagers generally face in America today, see Clark, *Hurt 2.0.*

CONCLUSION

While God's grace meets us in all sorts of ways—in reading and meditating on Scripture, on a walk through the beauty of creation, or even in watching a favorite movie—our claim in this chapter has been that God particularly shapes us through our relationships with others.[34]

Such a view is supported by the biblical stress on relationship and community. God is relational, revealed to us as Trinity and revealed through his gracious covenants with his people. God has also created us as relational, with the creation account providing a framework for the constant biblical stress on relating to one another. We are also shaped by relationships, a truth affirmed throughout Scripture and also confirmed through experience and the study of human community.

In Philippians 4, Paul appeals to his readers to think on "whatever is true, whatever is honorable, whatever is just, whatever is pure, whatever is pleasing, whatever is commendable . . ." (4:8). While such an appeal might lend itself to solipsistic reflection, Paul immediately follows with an encouragement to "keep on doing the things that you have learned and received and heard and seen in me" (4:9). Knowing what is virtuous and good and excellent comes throughout our involvement with others. Networks shape our faith.

PUTTING IT INTO PRACTICE

- Explore with young people the ideas they have about God. To what extent do they see God as distant, and to what extent do they experience God as relationally involved in their lives?

- Encourage young people to reflect on how they have already been shaped by relationships. Ask each young person to name five people who have significantly impacted them in life, and create a space to share stories about them.

- Challenge young people to think about the way they relate to others, and the impact they can have. As siblings, children, and friends to others, young people can already shape the lives of those they meet.

---

34. Such a claim is not intended to displace the importance of the means of grace, on which see chapter 2. *Networks for Faith Formation* provides a framework or setting within which such means of grace are embedded.

FURTHER READING

Dean, Kenda Creasy. *Practicing Passion: Youth and the Quest for a Passionate Church*. Grand Rapids: Eerdmans, 2004.

> Dean helpfully explores the importance of passionate faith for young people, and suggests ways in which the church can theologically and practically engage adolescents in the midst of the challenges they face.

Clark, Chap. *Hurt 2.0: Inside the World of Today's Teenagers*. Grand Rapids: Baker Academic, 2011.

> Drawing on a wide range of studies, Clark offers a description of the changing adolescent world within the United States, and points to the ways in which teenagers been abandoned by the adult world.

Peterson, Eugene H. *Practise Resurrection: A Conversation on Growing up in Christ*. London: Hodder & Stoughton, 2010.

> While not focused on young people as such, Peterson's reflective and prayerful engagement with Ephesians emphasizes the way in which God shapes us through relationships.

2

Bedroom Practices
Personal Faith

Character is formed through action, and it is transformed through action, including carefully planned and grace-sustained disciplines.

DALLAS WILLARD[1]

INTRODUCTION

A FEW YEARS AGO, while teaching in Singapore, I (Steve) invited the class to go on a field trip to study youth culture. The field trip allowed them in a few moments to see something of global youth culture, as well as the culture of a particular young person. In five minutes of careful observation, they would be able to explain some of the young person's personality, worldview, and faith. We set off on the field trip to my sixteen-year-old daughter's bedroom—with her permission of course!

Like most young people, my daughter's bedroom expressed her identity, her passions, and her hopes.[2] In fact, the bedroom is one of the first spaces within which young people are able to articulate and represent their social and cultural lives, their transitions, experiences, aspirations, and identities.[3] It is a key place where they think about life, write in their di-

1. Willard, *Great Omission*, 65.
2. Lincoln, "Feeling the Noise," 399.
3. Lincoln, "I've Stamped My Personality," 266.

ary, and pray. If teenagers create space in their lives for personal spiritual disciplines, it is often in their bedroom. For this reason this chapter uses the term "bedroom practices" to illustrate what young people do when they are alone to seek and to connect with God.[4]

This chapter will argue that personal practices of devotion are key ways in which young people—and, in fact, all people—grow spirituality, and will describe the way in which such bedroom practices help faith flourish. Since such practices orient the self to God, they open people to the Spirit and are a necessary network for helping faith grow. While other networks for faith formation involve relational bonds to others, bedroom practices are orientated to one's primary relationship with God.

We will also argue, however, that bedroom practices alone cannot sustain faith into adulthood. Unless supported by other networks, "bedroom faith" will wither away or become distorted. Church leaders, youth workers, and parents need to attend both to encouraging bedroom faith and to embedding it within a wide range of supportive relationships.

THE IMPORTANCE OF PERSONAL FAITH

While the Bible directs our gaze to the wider web of relationships in which faith grows, it also shows that God invites each of us personally into relationship. Each person, young or old, Jew or Gentile, is called to walk the way of faith.[5] This means that personal devotion, the root of bedroom faith, is essential. All God's people are called to obey God, a response to God that is particularly countercultural today.[6]

In the Old Testament, each person within Israel—and not just the priests and teachers—was called to such obedience. Children as well as adults, aliens as well as Israelites, were addressed by the divine command. God's call that "you shall be holy, as I am holy" (Lev 19:2) encompassed everyone in the community, so that the call to holiness in Leviticus is followed by laws that are for all.[7] In the postexilic period, Ezra's public reading of the

---

4. For a similar use, see the description of "bedroom spirituality" in Collins-Mayo et al., *Faith of Generation Y*, 32–51.

5. This becomes much more obvious in the New Testament than the Old, when followers of Christ had to count the cost before following the way of discipleship (Luke 14:25–33).

6. Willard notes, "The missing note in evangelical life today is not in the first instance *spirituality* but rather *obedience*" (*Great Omission*, 44).

7. As the Old Testament also makes clear, the failure of one individual within the

law was also before "all the people gathered together . . . men and women and all who could hear with understanding" (Neh 8:1–2).

The Old Testament also stresses that without obedience, sacrifice—and ritual purity—is worthless. While the ancient world was awash with sacrificial systems that assumed that the gods were placated through correct offerings, the God of Israel called for obedience to the law as necessary for true faith. God's word through Hosea, "I desire steadfast love and not sacrifice" (Hos 6:6), finds parallels throughout the Old Testament (Isa 1:10–15; Prov 21:3; Amos 5:21–24) and is later picked up by Jesus himself (Matt 9:13; 12:7).

The New Testament also emphasizes obedience—the "obedience of faith" (Rom 1:5; 16:26).[8] Faith—trust in God's work in Jesus—is that which binds us to God, and through which we find forgiveness and new life. Such faith is not simply a matter of accepting facts about God (Jas 2:19), but involves a trust that issues forth in obedience to God (Rom 6:1–14). Faith flows into obedience as God works in the lives of believers through the Spirit.[9]

The importance of personal devotion is also reflected in the biblical stress on purity of the heart. Within Scripture, the "heart" (Heb: *lēv*; Gk: *kardia*) is not simply the seat of the emotions but rather the center of each individual—the place where thoughts and desires reside and issue forth into actions.[10] The heart is the center of an individual's life.

The Old Testament as well as the New calls believers to love God with all their "hearts" (Deut 6:5; Mark 12:33). While the Old Testament prophesies that God will purify the heart in the new covenant (Jer 31:31–33), the New Testament traces the fulfillment of the prophecy in the giving of the Spirit to believers (Matt 26:28; 2 Cor 3:4–6; Heb 8:1–11). It is the Spirit that allows us to pursue God, the Spirit that works to draw us closer into union with Christ.

Jesus' teaching on purity in heart (Matt 5:8) calls for believers to obey the will of the Father rather than seek recognition from others. As Jesus teaches in the Sermon on the Mount, this will require pursuing faithful

---

wider community can bring judgement on all (Josh 7:1–26), and this informs later discussions of church discipline within the New Testament (1 Cor 5:1–5).

8. For a brief discussion of the role of faith in different New Testament books, see Schreiner, *Faith Alone*, 112–23.

9. For a particular helpful discussion of the biblical view of sanctification that emphasizes the centrality of union with Christ, see Smith, *Called to Be Saints*.

10. For a demonstration of this theme, see T. Sorg, "Heart," in Brown, ed., *New International Dictionary*, 180–84.

living, including prayer, almsgiving, and fasting privately, out of public view (Matt 6:1–18). Our secret practices before God help us to keep our focus on God rather than on others. Since it is the heart that is the root of our words and our desires (Matt 15:18–20), it is the heart that God needs to transform.

The devotion of the heart to God is also found in the rest of the New Testament. Paul rejoices that the Christians in Rome have become "obedient from the heart" to the teaching they had received (Rom 6:17), while salvation comes in part through believing "with the heart" that Jesus has been raised (Rom 10:9). The Spirit is given "in our hearts" as a promise of what is to come (2 Cor 1:22). Hebrews depicts the heart as that which needs to be strengthened by grace rather than by regulations (Heb 13:9), while the letter of James calls Christians to "purify your hearts" (Jas 4:8).

The image of the heart as that which is central to each person, then, highlights the personal dimension of faith. Unless the heart is devoted to God, being part of the faith community counts for little.

This is also a theme that was picked up by later theologians. John Wesley emphasized the importance of what he called "heart religion" in Christianity.[11] Without inner obedience to God, and inner conviction of God's love, Christianity can slide into nominalism, a religion with an "outward form of godliness but denying its power" (2 Tim 3:5). Wesley may have drawn on the insights of the Puritan John Flavel, whose treatise *Guarding the Heart*, stresses that "keeping the heart before God" is the calling of all Christians.[12] The Danish theologian Kierkegaard later mused on the same theme in his sermon *Purity of Heart Is to Will One Thing*.[13]

Within Scripture, then, true faith always involves personal devotion. Such faith is not individualistic, seeing religion as simply a transaction between the soul and God, but it is personally and existentially real. The search for authentic faith is a common theme among young people,[14] and one that picks ups the desire for a genuine encounter with God that also shapes the biblical narrative.

11. The theme occurs throughout Wesley, but is treated explicitly in his sermon, "The Circumcision of the Heart." For discussion of this theme in Wesley, see Sanders, *Wesley on the Christian Life*, 73–102; and, for an extended treatment, Clapper, *Renewal of the Heart*.

12. For a recent edition of this work, which was originally written in the seventeenth century, see Flavel, *Keeping the Heart*.

13. Kierkegaard, *Purity of Heart*.

14. The importance of authentic faith that is also passionate is a key theme of Dean, *Practicing Passion*.

THE VALUE OF PERSONAL PRACTICES

The Bible also sees personal devotion as reflected in spiritual practices. Such practices, disciplines, or habits can be categorized in a range of ways. Within Wesleyan theology, the means of grace include personal spiritual practices, such as prayer, Bible reading, fasting, and service, alongside corporate practices, such as worship, preaching, and Bible reading.[15]

In recent times, Foster's *Celebration of Discipline* has been highly influential, and has been followed by a number of publications encouraging growth in spiritual practices.[16] Foster distinguishes between inward disciplines, outward disciplines, and corporate disciplines, with inward disciplines including meditation, prayer, fasting, and study.[17] Willard, in contrast, distinguishes between disciplines of abstinence and disciplines of engagement, and sees key personal disciplines as including solitude, silence, and secrecy.[18] Whitney, from a Reformed perspective, offers a more traditional list, including prayer, Bible study, fasting, and journaling.[19]

Since the Bible offers no single list of spiritual disciplines, lists of such disciplines differ, but the basic point remains. Christians are individually called to live out their faith, to "work out their own salvation" knowing that God is working within them (Phil 2:12–13). Without such personal devotion, faith is dead and void. But with it, believers will see a growth in grace.

Theologically, it is also important to stress that spiritual disciplines are not a means to gain grace but a response to the grace that we have been given. We are declared righteous not because of our personal piety but because of Jesus' obedience to the Father, death for our sin, and resurrection to new life. As John Wesley stressed, Christians should not look at

15. For Wesley's discussion of the means of grace, see his sermon on the theme, "Sermon 16," and also Sanders, *Wesley on the Christian Life*, 173–90. Within Reformed theology, the means of grace have often been limited to the "objective means" by which God changes us; the (preaching of) the Word and the Sacraments (Horton, *Christian Faith*, 751–87).

16. More recently, Foster is also the founder of Renovaré, a movement that "provides practical resources for cultivating a life—the with-God life—that makes us like Jesus from the inside out" (Renovaré, "Training over Trying").

17. Foster, *Celebration of Discipline*. Foster also lists the outward disciplines as simplicity, solitude, submission, and service, while the corporate disciplines are confession, worship, guidance, and celebration.

18. For the full list of such disciplines, and a description of each of them, see Willard, *Spirit of the Disciplines*, 156–92.

19. Whitney, *Spiritual Disciplines*.

spiritual disciplines as the focus of their devotion, but rather to God, who graciously uses them to draw us to him.[20] Nonetheless, spiritual disciplines or practices allow us to live out the new life we have been given.

While studies of spiritual formation offer biblical and theological grounds for spiritual practices, sociological studies have demonstrated the way in which bedroom practices nurture and nourish faith development. Those who live out their faith through spiritual practices are more likely to grow in their faith, as studies of prayer and studying the Bible demonstrate.

The practice of prayer is, of course, a fundamental spiritual discipline of the Christian life. Throughout Scripture, God calls his people to pray, while the Psalms provide a vocabulary of prayer for readers and hearers of Scripture. Jesus' model prayer, called the Lord's Prayer (Matt 6:9–13; Luke 11:2–4), has also shaped prayer for the church, while the early church repeatedly emphasized the transforming power of prayer.[21] Prayer is at the heart of Christian life.

Studies of prayer among Christian youth have shown that there is a clear relationship between frequent prayer and "spiritual health."[22] Those who prayed daily were more likely to consider the church important and the Bible as relevant to their life, as well as believing in God. They also were more likely to feel supported by family and friends.

Prayer is also an example of a spiritual practice widely embraced outside the church. Both in America and in more secularized Britain, studies show that the vast majority of young people pray.[23] Prayer outside the church has benefits for the health of practitioners. Adolescents who prayed regularly felt more comfortable with life, including school. Prayer served as a protective agent against anxiety and stress.[24] A positive correlation was found between the frequency of adolescent prayer and their sense of purpose in life,[25] as well as positive attitudes toward school.[26]

20. A point Wesley makes in "The Means of Grace" (Wesley; "Sermon 16").

21. There is no space here to offer a theology of prayer or survey of its various forms. For one helpful guide, see Keller, *Prayer*.

22. Francis and Robins, *Urban Health and Spiritual Hope*, 39–54.

23. Research in America found that only 15 percent of teenagers never pray, while 40 percent who do pray do so early (Smith and Denton, *Soul Searching*, 47). For similar results in Britain, see Collins-Mayo et al., *Faith of Generation Y*, 25.

24. Nooney, "Religion, Stress."

25. Francis and Evans, "Personal Prayer and Purpose in Life."

26. Montgomery and Francis, " Personal Prayer and School-Related Attitudes."

Christian youth who pray, then, are more likely to be growing in their faith, and also more likely to be part of a Christian community. Young people outside the church, however, also find prayer beneficial, and it may be that prayer is a bridge to engaging young people with broader questions of faith.

While almost all young people pray at some time or another, engaging the Bible is a specifically Christian practice. Such engagement can take many forms, but the distinction that Wesley adopted between "hearing, studying, and meditating" on the Bible remains useful.[27] The Bible testifies to its own significance within God's purposes; it is the "word of God" (Heb 4:12), the "oracles of God" (Rom 3:2), the means by which God addresses his people. While Jesus' citations of the Old Testament demonstrated his view of it as God's word (Matt 4:1–11; 5:17–19; John 10:36), the church also came to accept the New Testament as equally inspired, and, from the earliest period, accepted that engaging the Bible was a means of hearing and encountering God.[28]

In the US, where the majority of young people still identify as Christians, over one third of US teenagers indicated they read the Bible at least once a month, with one third indicating they never read it.[29] In the UK, research carried out by the Bible Society found that 50 percent of young people who identify as Christians read their Bible less than once a month, while just one in three read it a couple of times a week or more. Large numbers of children and young people indicated that they were unfamiliar with some of the central stories form Scripture, such as the Tower of Babel or the Good Samaritan.[30]

Despite the lack of regular reading of Scripture, most American teenagers believe that the Bible influences them, at least in some way.[31] The

27. Wesley adopts such a distinction in various sermons, including in "Sermon 16."

28. The process of canonization took some time, but involved recognizing the way in which God was already speaking through the Scriptures to the church. For a recent defence of the NT canon—and a claim that its authority was recognized early on—see Kruger, *Canon Revisited.*

29. Barna Group, "State of the Bible," 45.

30. In the study, 89 percent of young people were unfamiliar with the tower of Babel, while 61 percent were unfamiliar with the story of the Good Samaritan. For a summary of the Bible Society research, see Field, "Bible Literacy."

31. The study reveals that a majority of teens (60 percent) say the Bible has at least some influence on their lives. Among those, an equal number of teens say the Bible has a lot of influence (30 percent) or some influence (30 percent). Only one in five US teens say the Bible has no influence on their lives (Barna Group, "State of the Bible," 17).

frequency of reading Scripture also leads to a greater influence on the lives of teens. Ninety-four percent of teens who read the Bible each day agree that the Bible has a great influence upon their lives. Young people also report that reading Scripture has a much greater impact than just listening to it, reflecting the importance of this activity for their spiritual growth.[32] Those who do read the Bible do so because they also believe it brings them closer to God.[33]

The correlation of Bible reading to spiritual growth is also supported by large-scale studies of churches. One such study concluded that biblical engagement is the one practice that would help people at every stage of maturity to grow in faith.[34] A study of congregations that help young people grow in faith found that such churches deeply value the Bible, since "It's in the Bible that youth learn the story, the truth, that shapes the life of faith."[35] Preaching and teaching the Bible is, in fact, a key part in which the church shapes all people, including youth.[36] When the church's teaching flows into the daily life of youth, then a corporate practice is linked with a personal one, and further growth takes place.

Bedroom practices have clear value for young people. For Christians, personal faith practices are a way of spiritual formation, a response to God's grace, and a means of changing and growing in the Christian life. Christians who express their personal devotion through such practices are more likely to remain in the church, and such practices also have a positive correlation with health and well-being. Churches should, as part of their ministry and mission, encourage young people to pray and read Scripture alone in their rooms (Matt 6:6), as well as pursuing all the other personal practices to help faith grow.

32. Ibid., 17.

33. Ibid., 19.

34. Hawkins and Parkinson, *What 1000 Churches Reveal*, 19.

35. Martinson and Black, "Special Research Report," 49. One of the forty-four "faith assets" that help young people grow in faith is a congregational faith that "emphasizes Scripture" (44).

36. Edie, *Book, Bath, Table, and Time*, 93–125. Edie emphasizes the importance of Scripture for youth and offers a number of strategies for developing biblical literacy with young people.

THE LIMITS OF PERSONAL PRACTICES

While bedroom faith is vitally important for faith to flourish, it also has its limits. Unless situated within a broader ecology of relationships and networks, two key developments are likely to take place. Firstly, bedroom faith will dwindle since it is the support of the community of faith that makes the habits of such faith plausible and possible. Secondly, bedroom faith will lead to a subjectivist and individualistic approach to Christianity, leading young people deeper into the self rather than to the God who seeks to transform.

On the first point, it is clear that personal practice and communal participation, being part of a church, reinforce each other. In the next chapter we will explore in more detail the importance of the church, but here it is sufficient to note that church involvement will lead young people to take seriously the importance of personal faith. The correlation between prayer or Bible reading and church involvement works both ways. The more people engage in these practices, the more likely they are to be part of a church; and the more they take part in church, the more likely they are to live out their faith in everyday life.

It is in church, after all, that young people find encouragement and support in living out their faith at home. It is in the church that young people will learn the language of faith to sustain them in the years ahead.[37] It is in relationships with other Christians that young people will find themselves inspired and encouraged to read the Scriptures, to learn what it is to pray in the name of Jesus, or to practice fasting over Lent. It is in the context of faith networks that young people learn and inhabit the way of faith.

Without the networks of Christian relationships, it is likely that such practices will diminish. Although those outside the church also pray, those who are Christians pray more regularly and frequently than those who do not. Reading Scripture is also likely to wither without participation in Christian community. The practice of studying Scripture to encounter God, after all, only makes sense in the light of the story that the church tells.

A further weakness of bedroom faith, if pursued alone, is that it is likely to lend itself to subjectivist and individualistic approaches to faith. While spiritual practices may take place, they become divorced from the habitat of Christian community and become subject to distortions of the faith.

---

37. On the importance of helping children learn the language of faith, see Smith and Denton, *Soul Searching*, 267–68.

One such distortion, based on the findings of the National Survey of Youth and Religion in the United States, is named by Christian Smith as "Moralistic Therapeutic Deism."[38] In such a worldview, God is seen as a distant and generally uninvolved deity who only intervenes to solve particular problems, while the goal of life centers on seeking happiness and feeling good about oneself. God's will for life is primarily moralistic—being nice and fair to others. As Smith notes, Moralistic Therapeutic Deism is "parasitic" on the mainstream religious traditions but ultimately inconsistent with their particular claims.

While in Britain there has not been a large-scale study of teenage religiosity that parallels the American National Survey of Youth and Religion, there are a number of different studies that show how young people approach and appropriate faith. One such study, focusing on the spirituality of young people born in the 1980s and 1990s (generation Y), concluded that most adopt what the researchers named as a "happy midi-narrative." This happy midi-narrative defines the goal of life as achieving happiness, and sees such happiness realized through self, family, and friends, but without the need for God.[39] Another study has also shown that although young people without any connection to a faith community will also pray, such young people will also be more open to horoscopes, fortune tellers, and contact with the dead.[40]

In terms of bedroom faith, pursuing spiritual practices without the support of wider networks can mean that young people adopt such practices as a means of feeling good and being happy, rather than as a means of conformity to the God revealed in Jesus. It is a travesty that such an approach to faith is sometimes encouraged by the church,[41] but it also the case that without the church to offer a different narrative of faith, young people exploring Christianity are unlikely to move beyond an individualistic understanding of faith.

While bedroom faith is essential for Christians—and, as argued earlier, reflects a key scriptural theme—its limits should also be taken seriously.

38. Ibid., 162–63.

39. Savage et al., *Making Sense of Generation Y*, 35–42.

40. Francis and Robbins, *Urban Hope and Spiritual Health*, 148–51.

41. One of the troubling conclusions of Smith's study was that Moralistic Therapeutic Deism was adopted or assumed by more than 50 percent of churchgoing young people, though significant exceptions did exist. Since Smith, a number of writers have sought to help churches combat the existence of MTD within their ranks. See, for example, Dean, *Almost Christian*.

God calls us not only to purify our hearts and live for him, but to take our part in the body of Christ, using our gifts and receiving the graces of others. While the lack of personal practices may lead to nominalism, their use outside the networks of faith can lead to subjectivist and individualistic approaches to God that fall far short of the Christian vision.

CONCLUSION

Bedroom practices are an important part of helping young people, and all Christians, own their faith. They are a necessary network for faith formation, crucial for spiritual growth. Unless faith is adopted in such a way that it gains purchase in and for the lives of individuals—unless it goes beyond church meetings and activities—it provides dry ground for the Spirit's work in producing fruits of grace in the lives of young people.

Bedroom practices, however, are insufficient for helping faith to develop. Unless young people are nurtured in a wider web of relationships and networks, spiritual practices can wither or become channels for an individualistic spirituality.

Bedroom practices should be encouraged, but should also always be situated within a wider cluster of other networks, including the fellowship of the church.

PUTTING IT INTO PRACTICE

- Encourage young people within your church to reflect on what their bedroom reveals about their values, preferences, and ideals. This could lead to a discussion of how we are shaped by culture, and how our faith might be reflected in our personal lives.

- Discuss with young people the spiritual practices that they find most helpful in growing as Christians. What is it that really helps them grow? Explore the way in which God's grace comes before our own response.

- Lead a series on some of the key Christian habits that help us grow. You might, for example, lead young people in a discussion of prayer, fasting, and almsgiving—the three habits of grace Jesus points to in Matthew 6.

FURTHER READING

Dean, Kenda Creasy. *Almost Christian: What the Faith of Our Teenagers is Telling the American Church.* Oxford: Oxford University Press, 2010.

Dean offers a helpful summary of the National Study of Youth and Religion, and explores ways that the church can help support its young people.

Whitney, Donald S. *Spiritual Disciplines of the Christian Life.* Rev. ed. Colorado Springs, CO: NavPress, 2014.

Whitney offers a practical workbook of key disciplines for the Christian life, including prayer, Bible reading, and fasting.

Willard, Dallas. *The Spirit of the Disciplines: Understanding How God Changes Lives.* New York: HarperCollins, 1988.

Willard offers a theological framework for understanding spiritual disciplines while also identifying key practices that can help disciples grow in faith.

3

The Church
Formation in Faith

The vision for spiritual maturity and holiness in the New Testament is distinctly *ecclesial*: the transformation of God is effected in our lives through the grace and witness of the church.

Gordon T. Smith[1]

INTRODUCTION

WHAT IS IT ABOUT the church that so many people—and not just the young—dislike? Why is it that younger people are more likely to rate experiences outside the church as more significant for their spirituality than those times when congregations gather around Word and Sacrament?

Sixteen-year-old Emily, for example, described her experience at Glastonbury, a UK music festival, as the greatest worship she had experienced. The church, in contrast, seemed to offer little, and so Emily stopped attending at age fifteen. As Emily explained,

> People of all ages gathered at Glastonbury, we all wanted to be there; we were lifted beyond ourselves and brought together all at the same time. Church isn't like that, it's routine. Many people don't want to be in church, they don't enjoy what's happening there, they just go because they feel they have to please God. I can't

1. Smith, *Called to Be Saints*, 191.

imagine anything happening in church that could be relevant to my life.[2]

Emily is not alone. In the United States, nearly six in ten (59 percent) young people who grow up in churches end up walking away from either their faith or the institutional church. The number of millennials who are "unchurched" has also increased in the last decade, from 44 percent to 52 percent, mirroring a larger cultural trend away from churchgoing among the nation's population.[3]

In Britain, recent research in the Church of England has shown that the decline of the church is due far more to loss of children and youth than to its failure to evangelize.[4] There has been a steady decline of young people across the denominations. Britain has now reached a point where more young people than not identify as non-religious.[5] Although the non-religious include many who still embrace spirituality and faith, the loss of the young within the church is still bad news.[6]

Against the backdrop of church decline, our aim in this chapter is to show that the church is a necessary network for faith formation. The church is not simply an antiquated institution or an optional addendum for Christian living. It is, rather, the "household of God . . . the pillar and bulwark of the truth" (1 Tim 3:14). Without it, faith cannot survive.

We begin by exploring biblical images of the church that point to its God-given identity to nurture and nourish us in the life of faith. We next summarize sociological evidence that points to the importance of church in building faith. Finally, we will explore how church participation shapes the faith of young people, and how churches can be more intentional in shaping their worship and their teaching to draw people closer to the living God.

2. Emery-Wright, *Now That Was Worship*, 5.

3. Barna Group, "5 Reasons Millennials."

4. As reported by the analysis of changes in church membership by the "Church Growth Research Programme" within the Church of England. See Voas and Watt, "Church Growth Research," 2, 14–25.

5. This was one of the conclusions from a YouGov poll commissioned by Linda Woodhead in December 2015. For a summary of the report, see Lancaster University, "Why 'No Religion.'"

6. While we have pointed to America and Britain in our examples here, a similar trend is happening across Europe (Voas, "Rise and Fall of Fuzzy Fidelity") as well as in Australia, New Zealand, and Canada. It is in the economically developed world where churches are most struggling to pass on faith.

THE CHURCH IN SCRIPTURE

The Bible uses a range of images of the church, all of which point to it as a necessary and vital means of growth for God's people. One author has identified ninety-six images of the church within the Bible,[7] and it is also possible to identify distinct ecclesiologies within the different voices of Scripture.[8] Rather than offering a complete biblical ecclesiology, we will here draw attention to three dominant images of the church: the family, the body of Christ, and the temple of God. Each image communicates something important about the church and can shape our understanding of why the church is so important for Christian faith.

The first image is that of the church as a family.[9] While having some precedents in the Old Testament,[10] this image of God's people becomes particularly prominent in the New Testament—including in the teaching of the gospels. Jesus encouraged his disciples to address God as "Father" (Matt 6:9–13) and identified those who followed him as members of his family (Luke 8:20–21). The family of God takes priority over earthly families, while Jesus taught that those who love their earthly families more than God risk forsaking the kingdom (Matt 10:37).[11]

Other New Testament writers develop the theme. In John's gospel, salvation involves birth "from above" (John 3:3–8), but being born in God's family comes through God's will rather than human decision (John 1:12–13). Paul similarly speaks of the adoption of believers into God's family (Rom 8), and addresses Christians as siblings throughout his letters (Rom 1:13; 12:1; 1 Cor 1:10; Gal 1:2; Phil 1:12).

The image of the church as a family points to its significance as the primary place of formation and fellowship in Christ. As one author puts it, "The church is God's most important institution on earth. The church

7. Minear, *Images of the Church*. For a more recent treatment of New Testament ecclesiology, see Ferguson, *Church of Christ*. The following discussion draws on three key images that we see as crucial in communicating the importance of the church.

8. This is not to say that a synthesis of such images is unimportant, even if different parts of the canon give priority to distinct images or models.

9. For a work that explores the significance of this image in the New Testament, see Hellerman, *When the Church Was a Family*. See also Ferguson, *Church of Christ*, 114–21; and Banks, *Paul's Idea*, 47–57.

10. See, for example, the reference to Israel as the "son" of Yahweh (Exod 4:22–23; Hos 11:1; Jer 31:9).

11. For the way in which Jesus' radical teaching on the family challenges the family values of many Christians, see Clapp, *Families at the Crossroads*.

is the social agent that most significantly shapes and forms the character of Christians."[12] But the image of the family also points to the church as a place of love and care for all, including those without natural families, the orphans and widows of the ancient world (Deut 14:28–29; Ps 82:3; Jas 1:27). The church as family can support young people as they grow, spiritually, emotionally, and relationally.[13]

A second image of the church, associated particularly with the apostle Paul, is that of the body of Christ.[14] While the image takes on more mystical overtones within the later Pauline letters, its use in Romans and 1 Corinthians draws on the political use of the metaphor but focuses on relationships within the church (Rom 12:3–8; 1 Cor 12:12–31). In Romans 12, Paul uses the image to show that each person within the body has gifts to offer to others (12:4–8). Since each member needs the other, recognizing the gifts of others brings humility (12:3). While gifts differ according to the grace that God has given (12:6), all serve to build up the church.

In 1 Corinthians 12, Paul similarly points out that the body of Christ has many members, all of whom need one another (12:12–13). Those who have public gifts need to remember their dependence on others (12:14–21), while those who seem to have weaker gifts need to know that they too are indispensable, and especially honored (12:22–24). God has so arranged the church, Paul argues, so that its members care for one another. If one member suffers, all suffer with them; if another rejoices, all share their joy (12:25–26).

The image of the body of Christ, then, points to the need for church to be a place of diversity within unity. Old people need the young; women need men; the rich need the poor. If we are all one in Christ, then we need to show this to the watching world. Our unity is threatened if the divisions within society are allowed to infringe within the church (1 Cor 11:17–23; Gal 3:28).[15] The image also points to the way in which every member of the body can contribute something to the whole. When young people are

---

12. Ibid., 67–68.

13. Dean points out that belonging to a community was a key part of "generative faith" among highly devoted Christian teenagers, alongside claiming a creed, pursuing a purpose, and harbouring hope (*Almost Christian*, 61–84).

14. On the "body of Christ", see Ferguson, *Church of Christ*, 91–103; Banks, *Paul's Idea*, 58–66.

15. For a popular exploration of the importance of diversity within the church, see McKnight, *A Fellowship of Differents*.

encouraged to share their gifts and graces with the church, they are more likely to stay involved and bless the wider body.[16]

The third image of the church is the temple of God. While explicitly used in Paul (1 Cor 3:16–17; Eph 2:19–21), it is also implicitly used throughout by other New Testament writers (John 2:19–25; cf. Rev 21).[17] In the Old Testament, the temple was the site of God's presence, a sphere where people could encounter and worship God. When applied to the church, the image of the temple highlights that the regular gathering of God's people is a site of God's powerful and real presence.

While the temple imagery is applied to the church, it also provides a horizon for the church's mission.[18] The church is the site of God's presence and, equipped by Word and Sacrament, Christians are sent out to bear that presence in whatever place they find themselves. Just as the church is a site of God's presence within the world, so the new heavens and the new earth will be full of God's presence (Rev 21–22). As Beale puts it, "the Church's place in the eschatological redemptive-historical story is that of being the inaugurated temple, which is designed to expand and spread God's presence throughout the earth."[19]

The image of the temple is a powerful reminder that church is a place where God is present (1 Cor 14:24–25). It is not simply a place to meet with friends, to learn information, or to go through ancient rituals, but a place where we meet God. This does not mean that people always *experience* a "spiritual high" within the church,[20] but it does mean that God has promised his presence within the midst of his people. The Exemplary Youth Ministry Study found that having a palpable sense of the presence of God correlates with the developing faith of young people.[21] Similar research in

16. On the importance of involvement within the church for young people, see Lytch, *Choosing Church*, 24–44. Lytch argues that teens are attracted to religious institutions that provide a place of belonging, a way to make meaning in their lives, and a challenge to develop competence in participating within the adult world.

17. For an argument that temple imagery is found throughout all the New Testament witnesses, see Beale, *Temple and the Church's Mission*. For further discussions of the temple in the New Testament, see Ferguson, *Church of Christ*, 125–29.

18. See Beale, *Temple and the Church's Mission*, and, for a briefer argument, Beale "Eden, the Temple."

19. Beale, "Eden, the Temple" 30.

20. For a critique of worship that simply seeks a "spiritual buzz" among young people, see Edie, *Book, Bath, Table, and Time*, 33–38.

21. Martinson and Black, "Special Research Report," 44.

the UK has shown that when young people do not sense the presence and power of God in worship, they stop attending.[22]

These images of the church—family, body of Christ, and temple—are not the only images within Scripture, but they highlight dimensions of the church that are particularly relevant for young people. As a family, the church supports and nurtures the young people within its midst. As the body of Christ, the church is a place where all can exercise their gifts. And as the temple of God, the church is a place of divine encounter, a site where God's presence is truly known.

The church, then, is necessary for faith formation; a God-given site where we grow in faith and love. Within a context of individualism and suspicion towards all institutions, the voice of Scripture needs to be heard afresh.[23] The church is central in God's plan. We cannot do without it. Apart from it, it is hard to form faith.

THE CHURCH AND FAITH

While Scripture highlights the importance of church for faith, studies of church attendance link it to a range of positive personal and social values, while also confirming that those who attend church are most likely to see faith grow.

The research of Robin Gill and Leslie Francis in Britain has demonstrated the social significance of church attendance in shaping a range of personal and social values.[24] Their studies show that church attendance offers significant protection against suicide, fosters an enhanced sense of purpose in life, and encourages the idea that we can have an effect on the world. Church attendees also display less racist attitudes and show a concern for world needs, such as poverty and the plight of refugees. Church attendance is good for the young person, good for the community, and good for the world. These are all key issues when it comes to spiritual health and growth.

22. Emery-Wright, *Now That Was Worship*.

23. While there are diverse views of the church, an understanding of the church as "one, holy, catholic, and apostolic" has won wide acceptance across all church traditions. For a discussion of these "marks," see Oden, *Classic Christianity*, 720–64, and, from a youth work perspective, see Matt Brain, "The Church," in Nash and Whitehead, eds., *Christian Youth Work*, 130–40.

24. Gill, *Church Going*; Francis and Robbins, *Urban Hope and Spiritual Health*; Francis, "Implicit Religion, Explicit Religion."

Studies in America also show that church attendance is correlated with a higher quality of life. Those who attend church are more likely to pursue education, to avoid drugs, and to remain committed to their faith in later life. The life outcome of religious teens—those who engage with a faith tradition—is better than those without religion.[25]

As pointed out in chapter 2, church attendees are more likely to engage Scripture and regularly pray. Practices of bedroom faith and church attendance are mutually reinforcing. Expressing a public faith through church participation helps Christians to maintain a personal faith. As one study of emerging adults puts it, "those who do sustain strong subjective religion in their lives, it turns out, are those who also maintain strong external expressions of faith, including religious service attendance."[26]

FORMING FAITH IN THE CHURCH

If Scripture points to the church as a network for faith formation that can help us develop and grow in faith,[27] how exactly should we understand the relationship between participation in church and growing in faith? What is so important—or necessary—about this particular network?

There are, we suggest, two areas where the church can particularly help young people develop in faith: through worship and through intentional faith formation. While each area happens through church in one way or another,[28] thinking about how such processes shape young people can help churches reflect more deeply on their own structures and practices, and perhaps restructure them so that they can help young people flourish.

The first area, formation through worship, can be explored through the "liturgical pedagogy" of James K. A. Smith.[29] For Smith, Christians

25. Smith and Denton, *Soul Searching*, 218–58.

26. Smith and Snell, *Souls in Transition*, 262.

27. Recent research on the "invisible church," those Christians who retain their faith without attending a church, may problematize our assertion (Aisthorpe, *Invisible Church*). While the research shows that there are such Christians, however, it also depicts them as often meeting with other Christians, showing the need for at least some form of Christian community to sustain faith.

28. See Eisner's discussion of the "explicit," "implicit," and "null" curriculum in Eisner, *Educational Imagination*. Even if faith formation does not happen explicitly, there will be implicit ways in which the church shapes the faith of its members—or even areas where there is little formation that takes place ("null" curriculum).

29. Smith has published two volumes of his "cultural liturgies" that sketch out this

have for too long approached faith intellectually, believing that thinking the right thoughts about God is what leads to growth in faith.[30] While encouraging biblical and doctrinal literacy is an important task,[31] it can lead to the misleading assumption that thinking rightly is what will change us. This can even lend itself to a faith that hardly needs the church; if we have figured out the doctrine, why do we need to keep attending church? It can ignore the central role of love and desire within our lives, as if to suggest that accepting truths is what Christianity is all about rather than the love of God.[32]

Smith argues, in contrast to intellectualist approaches to faith, that faith is developed far more through our habits and practices than through adopting a right worldview, and that the liturgy of worship is the way in which God works in and through us. A type of pedagogy is embedded in liturgy, as Smith demonstrates.[33] The rhythm of liturgy and worship shape us, even without us always knowing how, and so participation in church worship opens us up to this key way in which the Spirit works.[34] This, of course, needs to be embedded within Christian lives that seek to encounter God and love neighbor daily, but worship within the church remains central for all faith formation.[35]

Given the importance of worship, the church needs to empower young people to understand the shape of worship, and particularly the balance of Word and Sacrament within the church.[36] If God has indeed shaped the

---

"liturgical pedagogy": *Desiring the Kingdom* and *Imagining the Kingdom*. For his more accessible explanation to the role of practices or habits in the Christian life, see Smith, *You Are What Your Love.*

30. Smith, *Desiring the Kingdom*, 29–73.

31. Smith and Denton, for instance, argue that parents and church leaders need to teach young people about the faith (*Soul Searching*, 267).

32. Smith, *Desiring the Kingdom*, 75–88.

33. Smith's point finds support in the work of the anthropologist Roy Rappaport, who argues that worship shapes people and society in a way that words cannot (Rappaport, *Ritual and Religion*).

34. Smith, *Desiring the Kingdom*, 134–55. As Smith puts it, "The church's worship is a uniquely intense site of the Spirit's transformative presence" (150).

35. Smith notes that "Sunday worship" *alone* is insufficient to nurture Christian faith unless it is embedded within a whole set of other relationships through which grace grows, and so points to the need for the worship of the church to link to the lives beyond the walls of the church (ibid., 212–14).

36. For an excellent exploration of how churches can help young people engage with the shape of worship, see Edie, *Book, Bath, Table, and Time.*

church, then church leaders can trust that worship can really transform young people. When young people can also participate in shaping worship within the church, in dialogue with the tradition, then this can also help them find a way of worship that is contextually appropriate while also faithful to the tradition.[37] The love and acceptance they experience in this setting greatly enhances the likelihood of a lasting, meaningful faith.[38]

Alongside worship, young people are also formed in the faith when they take part in opportunities for intentional faith formation. Such intentional faith formation, what was once called catechesis, is often missing from the diet of youth groups and Sunday schools, where there is often a temptation to entertain rather than educate, or to focus on the experience of God over the church's teaching of God.[39] On the other hand, faith formation can also fall prey to a "schooling model" of education, where the focus on learning truths is divorced from the broader life of worship and faith.[40]

Intentional faith formation needs to embrace doctrine as well as practice, worship as well as ethics. The loss of catechetical ministries within the church can, in part, be blamed for the loss of the Christian mind as well as Christian living within society. Failure to teach young people the language of faith means they are less likely to articulate it, and so less likely to inhabit it as formative within their life.[41]

While Smith's critique of worldview thinking could lead to a denigration of doctrine,[42] learning the truths of faith actually helps young people also learn what it means to be a faithful Christian. Doctrine, in this sense, is not a disembodied set of truth claims, but truths that compel us to live and act in particular ways.[43] As Vanhoozer puts it, "Theology is not merely theoretical, a matter of information and the intellect, but also theatrical, a

---

37. On this, see Emery-Wright, *Empowering Young People.*

38. Allen and Ross, *Intergenerational Christian Formation*, 189–203.

39. As Foster reflects, "When I visit congregations today, they often seem more involved in educating to enrich *the religious experience* of children and youth than to *nurture them as disciples of Jesus Christ*. More attention is given to what children *want* or *like* than to what children *need* to follow Jesus together through the challenges they daily face" (*From Generation to Generation*, 59).

40. For a critique of the schooling model of faith education—and for a call to integrate faith education more tightly with worship—see Murphy, *Teaching that Transforms*.

41. Smith and Denton, *Soul Searching*, 267–68.

42. Smith's concern, however, is not to downgrade thinking rightly about God, but to situate it in the broader context of loving God—a love that is developed through worship.

43. Vanhoozer, *Faith Speaking Understanding.*

matter of forming, transforming, and performing 'habits of the heart' that lead to action (i.e., works of love)."[44]

Faith formation can also help young people learn what it means to worship and to pray, and what it means to live rightly before God. In an age where idolatry is rife—as the gods of consumerism, entertainment, and militarism march across the world—teaching young people to "worship God, and God alone" is needful.[45] And in an age where morality is often an expression of individual choice, the church also needs to help its young people learn what it means to live faithfully before God.[46]

Worship and intentional faith formation go hand in hand, and both are important.[47] Both are part of the church's calling, and thinking carefully about how to help young people engage with them is part of the church's challenge today.

CONCLUSION

The idea of a solo Christian is foreign to the concept of faith in both Scripture and church history. Gathering together with other Christians for worship, support, and mission has never been an optional extra of the faith, and should not be so today.

The church is, in fact, a primary network that helps faith grow. In a context where even church leaders downgrade the significance of the church, our plea in this chapter is to realize the church as God's means of growing Christians. In particular, the church at worship—encountering God through Word and Sacrament—is a place where we meet God.

If young people are not experiencing the church as a place of encouragement, gift sharing, and encounter with God, then hard questions need

44. Ibid., xiv–xv.

45. For a call to reclaim discernment in response to such challenges, see Mahan et al., *Awakening Discipleship*; White, *Practicing Discernment*; and Gardner, *Mend the Gap*, 23–66.

46. One of the most pressing moral challenges for young Christians today is around sexual ethics, but parents and churches often do a poor job helping young people approach this with Christian wisdom (Regnerus, *Forbidden Fruit*, 209–14). For a book that aims to equip churches in this area, see Emery-Wright, *Understanding Teenage Sexuality*.

47. Murphy, for instance, points to the importance of "liturgical catechesis." While at times she collapses all catechesis into the act of worship, she recognizes that catechesis alongside worship is also necessary (Murphy, *Teaching that Transforms*). For a call to catechesis from an evangelical perspective, see Packer and Parrett, *Grounded in the Gospel*.

to be asked. While the church may need to explore the way it functions and worships, it may also need to invest in helping children and young people learn what it means to be part of the church, particularly through worship and exploring faith.

PUTTING IT INTO PRACTICE

- Explore the key elements of church with young people. In particular, take time to explain how it is that God uses Word and Sacrament to shape us.

- Discuss with young people their experience of church. When have they felt alive to God within worship? Allow young people to experiment with planning and leading worship. Discuss these experiences with the young people and see what both the church and young people learn through them.

- What does faith formation look like in your church? What is intentionally taught or modeled within the youth group?

FURTHER READING

Emery-Wright, Steve. *Empowering Young People in Church*. Cambridge: Grove, 2008.

> This short booklet aims to help churches empower young people to be "theologians, interpreters, and liturgists" who can help in the creation of worship.

Packer, J. I., and Gary A. Parrett. *Grounded in the Gospel: Building Believers the Old-Fashioned Way*. Grand Rapids: Baker, 2010.

> Writing from an evangelical perspective, Packer and Parrett call for a return to catechetical ministry, demonstrating its importance within history and the potential for its renewal today.

Wilhoit, James C. *Spiritual Formation as if the Church Mattered: Growing in Christ through Community*. Grand Rapids: Baker Academic, 2008.

> While many books on spiritual formation acknowledge the importance of the church, Wilhoit's work explores how spirituality is nurtured within community.

4

Families

Foundations for Faith

Families do matter in determining the moral and religious outcomes of young adults, and they matter a great deal.

VERN L. BENGTSON[1]

INTRODUCTION

CHURCHES LOVE TO TELL stories of dramatic conversion. Within youth groups, such stories show that Jesus really changes lives, and so draw young people into the faith. Teenagers love stories of returning prodigals—the drug dealer who encounters Christ on the floor of a police cell, the sex worker who finds welcome and salvation through the witness of a Christian, or the hardened criminal repenting from sin and changing his life.

Such stories should, of course, be celebrated. And the church has a stock of such stories, with the most memorable examples including the apostle Paul and, later, Augustine of Hippo.[2] Such stories show that God's grace can change anyone.

1. Bengtson, *Families and Faith*, 195.

2. Paul's story is told in the Acts of the Apostles (9:1–9; 22:6–11; 26:12–18), but Paul also refers to his conversion in his Letter to the Galatians (1:13–17). While some scholars draw away from the language of conversion—Paul did, after all, remain a Jew— "conversion" is still an appropriate term for the dramatic transformation of Paul (Segal,

And yet stories of radical conversation can hide the truth that God typically works through families and the home, and that growing up in the faith is a huge blessing and privilege for Christian young people. If we always celebrate the grand stories of conversion, we can miss the ordinary ways in which God works. We can suggest to young people that real conversions require drama and fireworks, and that homegrown faith is somehow less valuable.

But faith nurtured within the home should be hugely valued. Those young people who remember following Jesus from their earliest age are a blessing to us all. They demonstrate that God works through families, and that the treasure of faith can be found in the young as well as the old. What else would we expect from a Lord who promises that the "first will be last and the last will be first" (Mark 10:13–16), and who blesses the children that his disciples thought to turn away (Matt 19:30)?

In the second century CE, we see the fruit of a childhood faith reflected in the story of Polycarp, the bishop of Smyrna. Polycarp had been brought up within the church, nurtured and trained in the faith at home, before later in life becoming a bishop.[3] During a period of persecution, Polycarp, by then in his eighties, was hauled before a Roman governor and asked to deny his faith and burn incense to the emperor. With outstanding courage, Polycarp responded with the words, "For eighty-six years I have been his servant, and he has done me no wrong. How can I blaspheme my King who saved me?"[4] The formation that began in Polycarp's childhood prepared him for his death many years later.

Being brought up within a Christian family can lead to an adult faith that lives with passion and courage, which takes faith to its heart and lives it out in the world. Families are, in fact, the primary network for building the faith of young people. This does not mean that young people do not become Christians in non-Christian homes but rather that families typically play the crucial role in the formation of young people's faith.[5] Churches desperately need to recognize this.

Paul the Convert). Augustine tells of his own conversion in his *Confessions*.

3. The claim of Polycarp to have served Christ for eight-six years (see below) suggests that he would have been brought up in the faith.

4. Polycarp, *Martyrdom* 9.16–17, in Holmes, *Apostolic Fathers*, 235.

5. Having both come to faith in Christ from non-Christian—though churchgoing—homes, we are both examples of exceptions to the rule, though for each of us members of our wider families have been crucial in helping faith grow and develop.

We begin by exploring the importance of families within Scripture, noting that God's work through families, embedded within the church, is a primary means for passing on faith. We will then show how social science depicts the significance of family for the values and faith commitments of children, before moving to a specific discussion of families and faith formation. We end the chapter with some final suggestions of how churches can encourage families to help their children and young people to learn and inhabit faith for themselves.

FAMILIES IN SCRIPTURE

The significance of families within God's purposes is established in the first chapters of Genesis. In the second creation narrative, God declares that "it is not good" for Adam to be alone and promises a helper for him (2:18),[6] so creating Eve from Adam's rib (2:21). Eve shares the same flesh and is created in the same image of God (Gen 2). Eve complements Adam and, with Adam, hears God's voice and God's commission.

It is the creation of Adam and Eve for one another that explains why marriage is part of human culture. Men and women leave their parental homes and set up new ones (Gen 2:24). They become "one flesh," deeply united under God.[7] They are also called to "go forth and multiply" (Gen 1:28), bearing children as the fruit of their union. Children are seen as a sign of God's blessing and love (Prov 17:6), a heritage from the Lord (Ps 127:3–5).[8]

---

6. Commentators point out that the word used for "helper" (Heb: ēzer) does not imply inferiority, since the same word is also for God's relationship to Israel (e.g., Ps 33:20) (Hamilton, Book of Genesis, 175–76).

7. It is the unity of man and woman as "one flesh" that leads to such serious strictures against other forms of human sexual relationship. Jesus prohibits divorce on these grounds (Mark 10:1–12), though the discussion of the exception clause (Matt 19:8) has generated mush discussion. The New Testament also sees fornication and adultery as rupturing the "one flesh" of covenantal marriage. For a discussion of a Christian understanding of marriage, engaging with the key texts, see Grenz, Sexual Ethics, 57–77. For a discussion of Scripture and sexuality, with a particular focus on young people, see Emery-Wright, Understanding Teenage Sexuality, 109–55.

8. Such a theological perspective meant that Judaism and Christianity valued children highly, sometimes in contrast to their surrounding cultures. On Old Testament teaching on children, see Michael S. Lawson, "Old Testament Teaching," in Anthony and Anthony, eds., Theology for Family Ministries, 66–87. For early Christian opposition to abortion, infanticide, and exposure of children—all common practices in the

Late theologians emphasized the blessing of marriage as given to all, a theme reflected in marriage services today. While its expression differs from age to age and place to place, its practice, the union of man and woman for procreation, is found across human cultures.[9]

The Bible also points to family as key for faith development.[10] Such a view reflects most ancient views of family, in which parents, and especially fathers, had the responsibility for helping their children follow the household religion. Unlike the modern world, where faith is often privatized and where children are encouraged to choose their own path, most ancient culture saw children as inheriting the faith of their parents. Indeed, to depart or renounce the faith of one's father was to dishonor one's family.

In one of the most important passages on the topic, Deuteronomy 6:6–9, parents are instructed to help their children learn and live out the law of God.[11] Such an instruction directly follows the Shema, the central declaration of Judaism confessing the identity of God ("The LORD our God, the LORD alone . . .") and its commitment to love God with "all your heart, and with all your soul, and with all your might" (6:4–5). The call to confess God and to love God is to be taught to children, along with the entire teaching of the law. Parents are called to help children engage with the law in a variety of different ways, such as through repetition, conversation, and the placement of visual reminders around the home.

The Jewish festivals were times when families gathered together, and were also opportunities for passing on the faith. The regulations for Passover, for instance, gave opportunities for children to ask questions about the meaning of the festival (Exod 12:21–28 cf. Deut 6:20–25). When asked about what the rituals actually meant (Exod 12:26), parents were able to explain how they pointed to God's redemptive work in leading Israel out of Egypt. Similarly, Joshua 6 explains that the memorial of the stones in the

---

Graeco-Roman world—see Bakke, *When Children*, 110–51.

9. See Clapp's summary of anthropological observations on this point in *Family at the Crossroads*, 39–44.

10. On the broader role of families in the Old Testament and the New Testament, see Michael S. Lawson, "Old Testament Teaching," in Anthony and Anthony, *Theology for Family Ministries*, 66–87; and Melick, "New Testament Teaching," in ibid., 88–105. Clapp also offers a helpful discussion of the differences between "biblical" families and families today (Clapp, *Family at the Crossroads*, 27–47).

11. For a helpful analysis of this passage, and the way in which the whole of Deuteronomy speaks of raising children, see Patrick D. Miller, "That the Children May Know," in Bunge, ed., *Child in the Bible*, 45–62.

Jordan, marking the passing into the land of Canaan, could prompt a child's query and lead to a reminder of what God had done (6:5–7).The book of Proverbs also highlights the role that parents had in shaping the faith of their children (22:6; 29:13), with many of the sayings no doubt passed on within the home (6:20–23; 13:1; 23:22–25).

In the New Testament, a number of texts also point to the importance of parents raising their children in the faith. Paul explicitly calls fathers to "instruct their children in the Lord" (Eph 6:4), and his description of a Christian parent "sanctifying" their child—even when married to an unbeliever—probably refers to the influence a Christian dad or mum has within the home (1 Cor 7:14).[12] For this reason too, a believer should not divorce an unbeliever—unless, of course, the unbeliever abandons them (1 Cor 7:12–16). The Pastoral Epistles also highlight that those who are church leaders need to be good fathers within the home (1 Tim 3:4; Titus 1:6).

Despite the importance of the home, the New Testament differs from the Old in subordinating the importance of the family to the community of the church. The church, rather than the family, is the primary "household of faith."[13] Such a perspective is reflected in Jesus' teaching that members of his family were those who chose to follow God (Mark 3:31–35), and in his warning that prioritizing family commitments over the kingdom meant exclusion from salvation (Mark 10:37). At one point, Jesus also warns his followers that his kingdom will cause conflict even in the heart of families (Mark 10:34–36).

The Scriptures, then, treat families as God's gift, but also—in the light of the kingdom—as subordinate to the call of God. Those within families should not rest their trust and hope in the family, but in God alone. But parents should also seek to model their faith within the home, passing it on to the next generation.

FAMILIES AND FAITH

Popular folklore sees young people, and teenagers in particular, as shaped primarily by their friends and peers. Many see parents as hardly influential

---

12. See Thiselton, *1 Corinthians*, 108.

13. This is a point emphasized by Clapp, *Family at the Crossroads*. See also Hellerman, *When the Church Was a Family*.

at all. Studies show, however, that parents remain the most influential force in a young person's life.[14]

Research among British teenagers revealed that the majority of those interviewed considered their family as key to guiding and supporting their life, with over half naming their families as the most important thing in their life.[15] As they face life's changes, teenagers look to parents for guidance and advice.[16]

Parents also influence the faith of their children. The research of Christian Smith, for example, shows that most teenagers retain the faith of their parents,[17] while the longitudinal study of Vern Bengtson demonstrates the point across a number of generations.[18] As Bengtson shows, children tend to follow the faith of their parents, although the way that families model and communicate faith is crucial in helping it to take root in the next generation.

The classic trope of the rebellious preacher's kid may lead some to think that intensive faith is off-putting to young people, perhaps even driving them away from faith, but a deep faith demonstrated and communicated by parents is what has the most significant impact on the faith of young people. In fact, the way parents communicate faith in the home is the crucial ingredient in helping faith transmit to the next generation.[19]

While the home is a key network for faith formation, its effectiveness has been blunted by two key developments since the 1960s. Churches need to take these into account as they think of ways to support families,

---

14. Martin et al., "Religious Socialization," 169.

15. Collins-Mayo et al., *Faith of Generation Y*, 33.

16. Collins-May, however, also found that the quality of parenting was important. Teenagers with parents who do not provide stability and emotional support will tend look to other adults for support, while teenagers with parents who were emotionally absent were more likely to participate in risky behavior, such as drinking and early sexual activity (Collins-Mayo et al., *Faith of Generation Y*, 36).

17. Smith and Denton note that 66–75 percent of thirteen- to seventeen-years-olds describe their religious beliefs as similar to their parents (*Soul Searching*, 128–29).

18. Bengtson, *Families and Faith*.

19. The point is demonstrated in a number of studies, including Bengtson, *Families and Faith*; Mark, *Passing on the Faith*; Kehrwald et al., *Families at the Center of Faith Formation*, 53–79. The importance of modeling is explored in the next section, but see especially Bengtson's analysis of Mormon, Jewish, and evangelical families, all of which are more successful than other religious groups in passing on religious identity (Bengtson, *Families and Faith*, 168–83). For a helpful summary of recent studies, see also Mark, *Passing on Faith*.

and realize that many Christian parents will struggle to know how best to model faith within the home.

Firstly, the breakdown of families affects the ability of parents to pass on faith to their children.[20] As Bengtson notes, "divorce has a disruptive effect on parents' attempt to pass down a religious heritage."[21] One reason for this is that children may find it harder to connect to a faith community if they spend time split between different households. If one parent leaves the faith or adheres to a different faith then it will be harder still for parents to pass on faith within the home.[22] Single parents might also find it more of a challenge to find time for family worship within the household.[23]

Churches need to work harder to support families affected by family breakdown and divorce, and provide particular support for single-parent families in helping to model and demonstrate faith at home. For such parents, church, and the relationships within it become even more important. Children and young people within such contexts will have an even greater need for adult mentors and elders within their lives, and their parents will need encouragement to persevere.

The value of faith formation in the home has also been affected by the failure of Christian parents to model and teach faith in the home. In the US context, Christian Smith notes that many parents, as well as church leaders, have given up any attempt to teach the faith within the home, being content simply to expose their children to faith.[24] In a recent report on church growth in the Church of England, only 11 percent of Anglican parents saw passing on religious faith to their children as a priority—compared to 94 percent who identified "good manners" as a priority and 83 percent "tolerance and respect."[25] As the authors of the report note, "On average, people

---

20. Bengtson, *Families and Faith*, 113–28.

21. Ibid., 118.

22. Lytch notes that if both parents do not belong to the same church—which is likely in a situation of family break down—then this creates dissonance for the child or children (*Choosing Church*, 174).

23. This clearly does not mean that single parents cannot model faith in the home, and some of the best examples of modeling faith in the home we have seen are in the context of single-parent families. Sociologically, however, passing on faith as a single parent is more difficult than in a team of two.

24. Smith and Denton, *Soul Searching*, 267.

25. Among regular Anglican churchgoers, the figure raises to 36 percent (Voas and Watt, "Church Growth Research," 18).

who call themselves Anglican seem unconcerned about transmitting religion to the next generation."[26]

There are probably a range of reasons for this development. A lack of confidence in their own faith, for instance, may mean that some Christian parents are unsure about what it means to pass faith on to their children, or they may assume that their own influence on their children's faith is likely to be minimal. Parents might also assume that it is the role of church leaders and youth pastors to teach their children faith, an assumption reinforced by the tendency to separate age groups within the church and employ "professionals" to work with the youth.[27]

A further reason of parents' failure to pass on faith is likely to be the modern, and postmodern, emphasis on personal autonomy and choice.[28] Parents may believe that it is ultimately each individual's choice that determines their faith, and that it is their child's spirituality rather than any particular religious tradition that is important. They may also fear that teaching faith to a child will ultimately restrict their child's freedom to choose for themselves.

Churches need to challenge such a view. After all, parents already teach their children about beliefs and values, through the said and the unsaid, what they do and what they ignore.[29] Parents assume it is part of their role to guide their children in areas such as education and sports, reading and music, relationships, and vocations. Parents also teach their children about faith, but often by what they do not say. The failure to teach or model faith communicates that faith is really not that important—or, perhaps, that any faith will do. While there are clearly damaging ways to teach faith,[30] to avoid teaching and modeling faith means that children are less likely to take on that faith for themselves.

26. Ibid.

27. Foster notes that the loss of intergenerational ties is one of the four challenges faced by congregations today (*From Generation to Generation*, 47–73). A number of authors are now focusing on the key role of parents—supported by the church—in passing on the faith, such as DeVries, *Family-Based Youth* Ministry; and Allen and Ross, *Intergenerational Christian Formation*.

28. On this theme, see Lytch's discussion of Gidden's "post-traditional self" in Lytch, *Choosing Church*, 89–93; and the discussion of "therapeutic individualism" in Smith and Denton, *Soul Searching*, 173–75.

29. As Mark notes, there is no "neutrality" in the home when it comes to teaching about faith (*Passing on Faith*, 17–18).

30. Bengtson notes that the perception that parents are trying to force religion on them can undermine religious continuity across generations (*Families and Faith*, 182).

Churches need to work harder at helping parents to see their role in modeling and teaching faith. In fact, it is often the interrelationship between the home and the church that particularly helps young people take on faith for themselves.

FAITH FOUNDATIONS IN THE HOME

If modeling and teaching faith within the home is so important, how exactly do families do it? What might it look like?

For parents to model faith means demonstrating its relevance and vitality to life. It means showing that there is congruity between a faith that is professed and a faith that is practiced. It means showing in life and deed that faith matters.[31]

Parents model faith when their love of God shapes their whole life. It is demonstrated as children see their parents praying together, seeking to love neighbors and enemies, and reflecting on life and work through the lens of faith.

Our children can also challenge us live up to our faith! My (Ed) youngest son woke me up early one morning and, after tucking him back to bed, I began to walk back to my bedroom. I heard a voice call out after me, "Are you going to pray, Dad?" I realized then that my son had noticed my prayer habits, and I was challenged to rise early for prayer more consistently.

Modeling faith also means prioritizing Sunday worship within the family. In fact, a commitment to church as a family habit correlates strongly with a child keeping faith when they leave home.[32] If churchgoing is part of family culture, then a child and young person learns that the parents value it highly, and they can learn to value it themselves. Adolescents are most likely to embrace faith when their parents attend church and believe religion is important.[33]

When parents attend church without living out the faith, however, it means that children are more likely to reject their religion. While churchgoing still has a positive impact on the faith of young people, the lack of congruity between the professed faith of a parent and the life that they live

---

31. Powell and Clark, *Sticky Faith*, 175–91; Lytch, *Choosing Church*, 202.

32. Lytch, *Choosing Church*, 177–82. As Lytch points out, "Families who cultivate the collective understanding that "our family attends church" tend to produce teens who believe they should be there" (182).

33. Bader, "Do as I Say and as I Do."

makes it more likely that young people will leave the church when they reach adulthood.

For parents to model faith, they also need to teach children what it means to be a Christian.[34] They need to help their children understand what the faith involves and also how to live the faith. According to sociologist Christian Smith, it is the neglect of the teaching of faith by parents and church leaders that has led to the lamentable inability of young Christians to explain what they believe and why they believe it.[35] Rather than inheriting the rich Christian faith of the centuries, children who are not taught the faith can instead inherit an unworthy imitation.

One of the most effective ways of teaching the faith—the how as well as the what—is for parents to lead family worship, gathering together with their children to pray and read Scripture.[36] While rooted in the Jewish-Christian emphasis on the family as a place where faith is modeled, it has also been a feature throughout the history of the church. Figures such as Chrysostom, Luther, Calvin, Wesley, and J. C. Ryle all emphasized the importance of worshiping within the home.[37]

Recent sociological studies have also shown that the families most likely to pass on faith to their children are those that prioritize family devotions or family worship.[38] Significantly, however, the relationship of parents to children is also important. Bengtson's research showed that parental warmth was crucial for passing on faith, and that an emotionally distant dad was likely to have a detrimental effect on his child's faith.[39] Family worship in homes where parents behave with love and warmth to their children is key for passing on faith. While it can never guarantee that young people

---

34. See Dean's emphasis on the important role of parents in "translating" the faith to their children (*Almost Christian*, 109–30).

35. Smith and Denton, *Soul Searching*, 267.

36. In our view, prayer and engagement with Scripture are the key elements of family worship. Others suggest other features should be involved, such as singing and catechesis, both of which could usefully accompany Scripture and prayer. For stories of how Christian families in the UK worship together, see Mackenzie and Crispin, *Together with God*.

37. For a brief summary of the history of family worship, see Timothy Paul Jones and Randy Stinson, "Family Ministry Models," in Anthony and Anthony, eds., *Theology for Family Ministries*, 155–80.

38. Lytch, *Choosing Church*, 176; Bengtson, *Families and Faith*, 168–83.

39. Bengtson, *Families and Faith*, 71–98.

will remain Christians as adults, it provides a firm foundation for a future life of faith.

The importance of parents does not, however, mean that faith is any less a gift of God. God can and does bypass natural human relationships—and God can raise up children of Abraham from rocks, if he so chooses (Matt 3:9). But God's grace and human networks and relationships are not antithetical. The grace of God comes through human intermediaries, and the Spirit works through parents as they share and speak the gospel into the lives of their children.

CONCLUSION

The tendency to see faith as an individual choice has in many ways undermined the role of parents. Parents may teach and model all sorts of values and behaviors in the home while giving little thought to what it means to pass on the faith. Or they may see the church as primarily responsible for nurturing the souls of their children while ignoring their own important role in the task.[40]

Scripture, however, clearly sees faith as nurtured and nourished by parents. As those who have received the blessing of children, fathers and mothers are called to help their children learn the truths of God and create opportunities for their children to encounter God for themselves.

Parents are called to model their faith and teach it to their children, and incorporating family worship within the culture of a home is a powerful way to help young people grow in faith.

As with other networks of faith, families are part of a broader ecology of relationships through which God works. Families should not be seen as the ultimate network—after all, many of us come to faith from families that do not believe—but they should be seen as a key way to encourage the faith of our young people, and to pass it on to future generations.

PUTTING IT INTO PRACTICE

- Explore with young people the impact of their parents, grandparents, and other members of their family on their own faith journey. Spend time giving thanks for the way in which God has worked through them.

40. Dean and Foster, *Godbearing Life*, 79.

- Provide opportunities to encourage parents to consider how they model and teach faith in the home. One of the best ways of doing this is to share and hear stories of how other parents lead family worship or incorporate habits of faith within the home.

- If you are a youth minister, ask parents for their support and feedback in the youth program, and talk with them about how they might best be supported in modeling faith within the home.

FURTHER READING

DeVries, Mark. *Family-Based Youth Ministry.* Rev. ed. Downers Grove, IL: InterVarsity, 2004.

DeVries makes an excellent case for the importance of families within the church, while also encouraging the church to act as an extended family for the youth in its midst.

Garland, Diana R. *Family Ministry: A Comprehensive Guide.* 2nd ed. Downers Grove, IL: InterVarsity, 2012.

A detailed guide on family ministry that includes sections on the context of family ministry, the processes of family life, family formation, and leading family ministry.

Mackenzie, Ed, and Gareth Crispin. *Together with God: An Introduction to Family Worship.* Birmingham, UK: Morse-Brown Design, 2016.

This short introduction to family worship includes suggestions for getting started as well as fifteen stories of how families worship together across the UK.

5

Friends
Building Faith

Holy friends challenge the sins we have come to love, affirm the gifts we are
afraid to claim and help us dream dreams we otherwise would not dream.

L. GREGORY JONES[1]

INTRODUCTION

IN THE 1990S, THE sitcom *Friends* dominated the airwaves, both in America
and as an American export that traveled the world. Based on the relationships between six friends living together in New York, the show showed
that friends stayed together through all of life's challenges and joys, even in
spite of occasional conflicts and personal idiosyncrasies.

Like other sitcoms that came in its wake—such as *Sex and the City,
Will and Grace,* and *The Big Bang Theory—Friends* celebrated friendship as
a key relationship or network. The friends on the show were like a family
to each another.[2] As one writer noted at the time, *Friends* "taught that the
most important things in the world are to have a sense of humor and some
good friends."[3]

1. Jones, "Discovering Hope."
2. There was, of course, one family relationship within the *Friends* group: Ross and
Monica were siblings.
3. Sandell, "I'll Be There for You," 146.

As the past decades have seen unprecedented levels of family breakdown, friendship has become increasing valued in popular culture. While families are less and less stable, and lovers or spouses come and go, friends stick together. Friendship is a social glue that promises intimacy and purpose.

Friendship is also hugely significant for teenagers. As children begin their journey into adulthood, friends help young people create their identity. They also influence children for good or for ill!

At thirteen years old, I (Steve) spent a great day with friends playing at the gravel pits on a rope swing over a deep pit filled with water. On the way back home, we jumped from a bridge into a river. Both activities were fraught with risk; the gravel pits were next to a road where heavy trucks frequently drove, and the river was isolated and deep. The risk made it even more exciting! When I got home later that day, I apologized to my mum for being late, explaining I was out with friends at the gravel pits. Needless to say, she was angry. My retort was, "All my friends were doing it." My mum spoke more truth than she knew as she exclaimed, "If your friends jumped off a bridge, then, would you too?" "Of course," I told her, "I just did!"

As adults, we can think back to the significant ways our friends have shaped us, leading us to do things or try things that we would not have done on our own. As we grow throughout our teenage years, friends grow in significance. While parents remain important for teenagers, friends are a further network for faith formation, a means by which God shapes us. Friends encourage us when things are difficult, challenge us when we are in danger of straying from our convictions, and persuade us of the ongoing viability of faith.

In this chapter, we explore the importance of friendships for building faith. We begin by exploring biblical depictions of friendship before showing the role of friends in helping adolescents construct their identity. We then show the importance of friendships for faith formation, highlighting ways that churches, youth groups, and parents can take friends into account when thinking about the faith of their young people.

FRIENDS IN SCRIPTURE

Rather than offering theories of friendship, the Bible gives us stories of friends. While a theology of friendship can be unearthed from such accounts, one of the obvious points of such stories is that good friendships

FRIENDS

sustain and encourage the love of God and neighbor.[4] Particularly when
faith is under threat, it is friends who help those who trust in God to keep
the faith.[5] The lack of friends, then, is a source of lament and pain. Without
such friends, trusting God becomes far more difficult.

One of the most well-known friendships in the Old Testament is
between David and Jonathan.[6] David and Jonathan's bond was so strong
that they entered a covenant of friendship, an agreement to stick together
regardless of what came (1 Sam 18:1–2). Such a loyalty was tested when
Jonathan's father, King Saul, threatened to kill David. Rather than help find
David, Jonathan chose instead to warn his friend of his father's threats, saving him from death and hastening the end of his father's reign (1 Sam 20).

The intimacy of David and Jonathan's friendship is reflected in the
description of Jonathan's love for his friend. Jonathan "binds his soul" to
David, loving him as he did himself (1 Sam 18:1–2). It is also expressed
in David's lament after Jonathan's death, when David described the love
of Jonathan as "wonderful, passing the love of women" (2 Sam 1:26). This
is not coded homoeroticism,[7] but a declaration of the intimacy that they
shared as friends.

David and Jonathan's friendship represents, in a particularly intensive
form, characteristics of a good friendship, and particularly its capacity to
provoke love and loyalty. Such a friendship can provide a framework for
encouraging one another in the life of faith. Friends we trust can become
"soul friends," companioning in our pursuit of God.

Good friendships are also praised within the wisdom literature. A true
friend "sticks closer than one's nearest kin" (Prov 18:24), offers forgiveness
rather than dwelling on what's gone wrong (Prov 17:9), and speaks the
truth, even when it hurts (Prov 27:6). In contrast, false friends leave when
things get difficult (Ps 38:11; 41:9), and are often attracted only by what

4. While we do not explore the theme below, the Bible also depicts God's relationship
to us as a form of friendship. For reflections on that theme, see McCarthy, *Good Life*,
38–41.

5. On this point, see C. S. Lewis' comment that "Every real Friendship is a sort of se-
cession, even a rebellion" (*Four Loves*, 96). As Lewis notes, it was friendships that helped
early Christianity survive in a society where it was treated with contempt.

6. 1 Samuel 18–20. For other stories of friendship, see the depiction of Job's friends,
who are rewarded for being there for Job even if their advice left much to be desired (Job
2:11; 42:7–9). See also the friendship between Naomi and Ruth (Ruth 1).

7. The tendency to sexualize intimate friendship arguably makes the task of friendship more difficult, especially for men. For more on this point, see Lewis, *Four Loves*,
72–73.

they can gain from the relationship (Prov 19:4). The wisdom literature also warns against ungodly friends, those who would lead the righteous away from God (Ps 1).

In the New Testament, the gospels depict Jesus as a friend to his disciples, as well as their Lord. Jesus calls his disciples friends rather than servants, since he had made known to them his father's will and plan (John 15:15).[8] Peter, James, and John also feature as Jesus' inner circle of friends. It is these three who most often accompany Jesus at significant points in his ministry (Matt 17:1–11; 26:36–38). John's gospel also depicts Jesus' friendship with the "beloved disciple," a disciple who rests on Jesus at the last supper and passes on memories of Jesus to the gospel writer (John 13:23; 19:26; 20:2; 21:20).

In the depiction of Jesus' passion, we also see the failure of friendship. Jesus asks his disciples to stay awake as he prays in Gethsemane, but he is left to pray alone as he approaches his death (Matt 26:36–38). While Peter promises to be there till the end, he abandons Jesus out of fear for his life (Mark 14:29–31). The shepherd approaches his end, and the sheep scatter (Matt 26:31 cf. Zech 13:7). And yet Jesus also renews his friendship with the disciples after his resurrection. In John 21, Jesus powerfully recommissions Peter, inviting his declaration of love while declaring that he will become a leader of the early church.

The earliest Christian missionaries also seem to have been close friends. Although the word "friend" is not used, Paul's relationships with his coworkers, such as Timothy and Silas, are close and warm (Acts 15:40; 1 Thess 3:2). Paul's greetings to a number of people in Rome also reflect the qualities of friendship, with many of those named described as Paul's "beloved" (Rom 16:5, 8, 9, 12). Paul was friends with his coworkers, and such friendship sustained their time laboring together in passing on the gospel among the ancient Mediterranean communities.

Paul's encouragement to early Christians to love and respect one another, to look out and associate with the lowly, and to act with hospitality (Rom 12:9–16) also suggests that the early Christians churches were to be a company of friends. In fact, ancient readers would recognize much of the vocabulary that Paul uses in his letters as implying relationships of friendship, while several of his letters can also be designed as "letters of

8. John's gospel also sees such friendships sustained as Jesus' disciples keep his commands, and so are drawn into relationship with the Father, as well as the Son and the Spirit (John 15:9–19).

friendship."[9] Such friendship creates a context for Christians lovingly to speak truth to each another, and so help one another grow in faith (Eph 4:15–16).

Like the Old Testament, the New also warns the people of God against relationships that would leave them away from faith (1 Cor 15:33). At the same time, Paul warns Christians against removing oneself from the world (1 Cor 15:9–10), and encourages wisdom in relating to those outside the church (Col 4:5 cf. 1 Thess 4:12). While we might imagine that Paul would encourage young Christians to have friends outside the church as well as within it, Paul would also stress the importance of strong friendships in Christ. It is within the context of such friendships that Christians can "build one another up" in the way of Jesus.[10]

In his classic treatment of friendship, C. S. Lewis argued that it is often friendships that make life worthwhile, even if the experience of intimate friends is less common today than it once was.[11] Friends look together in the same direction, shaped by the same passions and interests. Such friendships are a gift of God that help us, whether young or old, sustain our faith.

FRIENDSHIP AND FAITH

As noted earlier, friendship is a particularly important network for young people. Friendships help teenagers develop their own distinct identity and so negotiate the transition to the adult world. Friends also strongly influence and shape the beliefs of young people, both for good or for ill. Social changes mean that such a network is perhaps more important today than ever before.

The importance of friendship in helping young develop their identity has been widely demonstrated in developmental psychology. As the seminal work of Erik Erikson has shown, adolescence involves the crucial developmental task of "individuation," a process through which young people begin to construct their own identity, and so answer the question, "Who

9. Johnson, "Making Connections."

10. Such friendships would likely be intergenerational, since teenagers and adults would not be segregated as much as they are today. Such friendships would also embrace mentoring relationships (see chapter 4). Dean and Foster, in fact, describe mentors as a type of "spiritual friend" (*Godbearing Life*, 129).

11. Lewis, *Four Loves*, 69–109.

am I?"[12] Such a question is fed by a combination of physical, cognitive, and social change, as well as the serious life choices that begin to emerge for teenagers. The process of individuation leads to a sharpened sense of one's distinctiveness and self-boundaries, and is reflected in adolescents taking responsibility for their own identity and actions. While Erikson's theory has been refined in places,[13] the basic process of individuation continues to be accepted in the field of developmental psychology.

In this phase of human development, the role of friends is particularly significant. While parents still play a key role in the lives of teens, teenagers increasingly shape their identity in relation to their peers, and particularly their friends. Friends help teens and emerging adults make sense of the world. They mirror back the possibilities for the self's own development, and affirm or undermine the self's own sense of identity.[14] Friendships can also provide a security blanket for exploring identity. Among younger adolescents, the security of friendship requires conformity to peer groups, expressed in style of dress, language, and even music.[15] Older adolescents, in contrast, are more open to diverse kinds of friends.

Friendships are also important because they shape personal beliefs and values. While this is the case for friends at other stages of life as well, the process of individuation means that the impact of friends on beliefs and values is far greater for teenagers. Peer influence, then, plays a crucial role for young people, and can be both negative and positive.

The negative effects of friendship and peer influence have been widely demonstrated in areas such as initial sexual behavior, cigarette smoking, negative body image, binge drinking, delinquency, and other activities.[16]

---

12. Erikson, *Identity, Youth and Crisis*. For reflections on the process of individuation from a theological perspective, see Jacober, *Adolescent Journey*, 49–73.

13. A number of theorists have argued that the process of individuation differs from culture to culture, with individuation taking a different shape in less individualistic cultures. In Asia, for instance, there is a greater tendency to internalize the expectations of authority figures (including parents) (Berman, "Identity Exploration," 66). In lectures I (Steve) delivered on individuation to Chinese youth workers in Malaysia, some of the youth objected to the term on these grounds. After some discussion, they felt that it *did* happen in Asia, but that it was expressed in different ways than in the States or Britain.

14. For the importance of others in forming the self during adolescence, see Dean and Foster, *Godbearing Life*, 41–53.

15. Such marks of conformity helps early adolescents distinguish themselves from their parents while providing a sense of security that comes from belonging to a group (Elkind, *Sympathetic Understanding*, 205).

16. Jones et al., "Friendship Characteristics," 54.

When parents are absent—physically or emotionally—the negative potential of friendships also increases. Young people may seek elder peers to act as parents as well as friends, and this increases the risks of friends shaping behavior for ill.

Friends can also, however, have a hugely positive influence on young people. In one study, the influence of best friends on adolescent "pro-social" behavior was investigated over a two-year period. The researchers demonstrated that friends provided positive influence in academics and social activities.[17]

Friends also shape belief, with the presence of Christian friends helping young people keep their faith.[18] In *Faith Generation*, Nick Shepherd argues that young people especially need to spend time with other Christian youth to keep faith "plausible" in a society in which faith is simply one option among others.[19] As less and less young people hold to Christian faith, youth groups and other times for young people to meet provide "plausibility shelters" in which the choice to believe can make sense. Christian friends provide examples of an alternative lifestyle and show that faith is possible even in a hostile environment.

Friendship is also an important network because the influence of friends on young people is greater today than perhaps at any time in the past.[20] There are a number of reasons for this. Family breakdown and the formation of new forms of family has meant that families have become less stable, with young people looking far more to peers rather than to parents for help in navigating life. Young people are also spending more time with their friends and their peers than within the home, often because both parents are working. The growing presence and use of social media is also a crucial recent development; young people can always be online with their friends, even in the midst of family or church activities. As the networked world continues to explode, we can expect to see friends continue to grow in significance.

While friends are key to identity, the possibility of finding a single, stable identity is increasingly undermined in today's postmodern society.

17. Barry and Wentzel, "Friend Influence."

18. Smith and Denton, *Soul Searching*, 116; Jones et al., "Friendship Characteristics," 64. The same is true for other ages too, as Stroope demonstrates in "Social Networks."

19. Shepherd, *Faith Generation*, 56–78. Shepherd's focus is particularly on the youth group setting, as it is there that friendships and relationships are nurtured.

20. Jones et al., "Friendship Characteristics," 55, 65.

Zygmunt Bauman has argued that contemporary consumeristic culture is "liquid," fluid and ever changing. Whereas adolescence once involved creating or finding a stable identity, Bauman argues that the liquid nature of the contemporary world means that young people are unlikely to ever discover a unified purpose in life, worldview, or identity. They will be different people in different groups, with a chameleon-like personality,[21] and identities that can swap and change as they age.

At a stage of life when young people are seeking a stable identity, or perhaps rejecting a solid identity in favor of perpetually changing images of the self, the church proclaims the gift of identity in Christ.[22] Such an identity, however, is always communicated in and through the very real and visible relationships that young people enter. Friendships are key for faith formation.

BUILDING FAITH THROUGH FRIENDSHIP

If friends are important, as we have argued above, how can youth leaders, parents, and all within the church create the good soil that nurtures friendships that build faith? How can the church encourage young people to see their friendships as a place of grace, a place where God is able to work in their lives?

Firstly, churches need to create multiple contexts for young people to spend time with other Christians, since it is in times spent together that friendships emerge. This, of course, already happens within most churches. Many churches run Sunday schools and youth groups, and encourage young people to attend camps and festivals as well. Parents also play a key role in this. It is parents who often guide and signpost Christian events for young people, and so the networking that parents do behind the scenes is a key way in which friendships are nurtured. As well as such settings, the church can help to create contexts outside of formal church activities for young Christians to meet together.

Times for youth should involve fun and friendship building, as well as Bible study, praying, and worshiping together. Enjoying games and activities together is not secondary or trivial to faith, but are opportunities for friendships to begin and deepen.

21. Bauman, *Liquid Life*, 6–8.

22. On the relationship between God's fidelity and adolescent identity, see Dean, *Practicing Passion*, 73–92.

The importance of Christian friends and peers is only going to become more important as the faith and values of the church becomes increasingly at odds with the surrounding society. It was the close relationships between the early Christians that helped them to remain faithful to the gospel,[23] and the same is likely to be true today as the memory of Christendom continues to fade. A network of good supportive friends who hold Christian values and practices affirm that walking faithfully with God is viable. This network of friends also provides accountability, creating a desire to avoid letting the group down or to go against its values.[24]

A second means to promote friendship among young people is to give them opportunities to participate more fully in worship, and so share the gifts that they bring. While much of youth ministry has historically separated young people from the worshiping community, a range of recent writers laments the cost of such separation, and rightly call for the reintegration of young people within worship.[25] As such integration takes place, young people should also be invited to participate more fully in the worshiping community and contribute to the worship.

While we have previously emphasized the importance of including young people in the worship of the church, here we note that such inclusion promotes and enables friendship. Research within the Methodist Church of Britain revealed that having friends share in worship creates a context where young people felt free to be authentic in their actions and responses.[26] Teenagers who were interviewed explained that having other young people present enabled them to expresses themselves with emotion, through tears, laughter, and even dancing. As seventeen-year-old Lauren put it, "With lots of other young people we feel comfortable and relaxed—we feel like we belong here and can be ourselves."

Having other young people involved in worship also gave young people scope to experiment with their engagement in worship and explore their identity as Christians. This was especially true in worship that the young people helped to create, but it was also true in intergenerational

23. A point that Lewis makes in his discussion of friendship (*Four Loves*, 69–109). This, of course, is not the *only* reason, but one significant factor, and one that overlaps with the way in which early Christians found a family in the church.

24. Adamczyk, "Friends' Religiosity and First Sex," 924–27.

25. Allen and Ross, *Intergenerational Christian Formation*, 189–203.

26. Emery-Wright, *Now That Was Worship*, 80–84. While the research was specifically on worship, it can be applied more broadly to the way in which the presence of peers helps young people with faith.

worship where friends were present. The presence of other young people in worship fostered an intimacy in which those present felt encouraged and accepted by peers and God.

The presence of peers in worship also helps teenagers see that God is really present and working in the lives of others. When teenagers observe their peers engaging with God they become more alive to the possibility they too can meet God. Being surrounded by worshiping friends motivates others to worship, in the same way that a person staring into the sky causes others to look up.

CONCLUSION

In his reflections on friendship, C. S. Lewis explains that friendship is often seen as one of the "lesser loves." It is less passionate than erotic love, less sacrificial than "agape" love, and less natural than affection.[27] And yet, it is often friendships that sustain us within life, that give us a sense of connection to others. It is among friends that we share together in interests and passions.

Within the church, the value of friendships for sustaining faith has perhaps been less emphasized than it should. While we have heard sermons that call us to demonstrate sacrificial love or encourage us to channel our erotic love into the right contexts, we have rarely heard sermons on the importance of friendship. But as this chapter has demonstrated, friendship is an important biblical theme. Being a loyal friend is a gift of God, and loyal friends can keep us faithful to following the path of the cross.

For teens in particular, friendships are hugely important. Parents and church leaders can create contexts where Christian friends can support one another, and so grow in faith. Such friends may be important for a time, or may last into the future. Either way, they help young people sustain faith in a context where it is increasingly harder to remain loyal to Christ, or see why God matters in crafting one's identity.

PUTTING IT INTO PRACTICE

- If there is a lack of young people within your church, then it is even more important to help them find Christians friends in other contexts. This

27. Lewis, *Four Loves*, 69–109.

might mean linking up with a local church, encouraging participation in camps and festivals, or, more intentionally, seeking forms of intergenerational friendship.

- Make sure your church programs are fun for young people, and include activities where they can laugh together and build up important memories. Take trips, watch movies, and put on game nights—the opportunities are endless.

- Be aware of the potential for negative friendships to shape the lives of young people. Sometimes teens need to be protected from the harmful influences of their peers, even if reaching out to such peers will be part of the church's mission.

FURTHER READING

Christie, Lee. *Unfinished Sentences: 450 Tantalizing Statement-Starters to Get Teenagers Talking and Thinking*. Grand Rapids: Zondervan, 2000.

These discussion starters are a helpful guide to encouraging conversations on faith and life among teens, providing fertile ground for friendships to develop and deepen.

Lewis, C. S. *The Four Loves*. London: HarperCollins, 1960.

Lewis' classic treatment of four kinds of love includes insightful reflections on the value of friendship.

Mayo, Jeanne. *Thriving Youth Groups: Secrets for Growing Your Ministry*. Loveland, CO: Youthsource, 2005.

While focused on growing a youth group, a key theme within Mayo's work is that of cultivating a friendship culture, and Mayo offers helpful advice on helping youth groups become places of welcome and friendship.

6

Mentors
Modeling Faith

The gift of mentoring helps transform mere chronology into sacred story, mere biography into spiritual autobiography.

KEITH R. ANDERSON AND RANDY D. REESE[1]

INTRODUCTION

JESSIE RARELY MISSED THE evening worship services that the youth group led, and she always attended the other events they ran. Although not an official leader, Jessie loved to spend time with the youth, and she spoke with them whenever and wherever possible. At eighty-five years old, Jessie was an unexpected mentor to teenagers in her church. Yet her impact was immense.

The influence of Jessie on the young people became obvious at her funeral, which took place in small New Zealand Methodist Church in the mid-1990s. The church was packed, and the congregation and youth group filled the pews and the back hall as stories were shared of God's grace working in and through Jessie's life. One young person spoke of how Jessie took the time to get to know him. Another shared how Jessie was such an example of living faith. Several spoke of the love that she had for them.

---

1. Anderson and Reese, *Spiritual Mentoring*, 41.

Jessie was a mentor for the young people in her church, an older and wiser Christian who invested in the lives of those younger in faith and life.

In a world where youth and adults rarely mix outside the family, mentors are a gift that the church can offer its youth. While parents give love and ongoing support to their children, mentors offer guidance and wisdom alongside friendship and a listening ear.

While there are a variety of definitions of mentoring, Christian mentoring can be broadly understood as the formal and informal ways in which one person encourages another in the life of faith.[2] Although it can occur between peers, mentoring typically takes place between an older person and someone younger in faith. Formal mentors intentionally set aside time to meet and encourage younger Christians, whether to disciple them, offer wisdom and guidance, or give them space to share and to talk.[3] Informal mentors, on the other hand, provide examples and encouragement to younger Christians, taking time to engage them in conversation and include them in activities.[4]

In this chapter, we begin by tracing the variety of mentoring relationships that exist in Scripture, including those between Moses and Aaron, Elijah and Elisha, Jesus and his disciples, and Paul and Timothy. We next turn to the value of mentors for youth development. Whether in church or

2. For a helpful and influential description of *eight* different types of mentoring relationships, see Stanley and Clinton, *Connecting*. Formal ways of mentoring encompass what Stanley and Clinton describe as intensive mentoring (the Discipler, Spiritual Guide, or Coach) or occasional mentoring (counsellor, teacher, sponsor). Informal mentoring describes what Stanley and Clinton describe as a passive mentoring relationship (contemporary or historical), with "contemporary" mentoring referring to people whose life or ministry indirectly empowers another person.

3. Much of the Christian mentoring literature draws a link between mentoring and spiritual direction. For one example, see Anderson and Reese, who define spiritual mentoring as, "*a triadic relationship between mentor, mentoree and the Holy Spirit, where the mentoree can discover, through the already present action of God, intimacy with God, ultimate identity as a child of God and a unique voice for kingdom responsibility*," *Spiritual Mentoring*, 12. In a helpful appendix, they also provide contemporary definitions of spiritual mentoring that include definitions of spiritual direction, making clear their equation between the two, *Spiritual Mentoring*, 202–6.

4. So-called "natural mentoring" can be seen as partly informal and partly formal. As an informal type of mentoring, the relationship between the mentor and the mentoree emerges organically and without much structure. As a formal type of mentoring, the relationship will typically include meeting together one-to-one, and a degree of intentionality that can be absent from informal mentoring relationships. On the importance of "natural mentors," see Lanker, "Life-Long Guides"; Lanker, "Family of Faith"; and Lanker & Issler, "Relationship."

in wider life, mentoring relationships between youth and adults are of huge value. Finally, we explore the role of mentoring in faith formation, suggesting two key ways in which churches can promote mentoring as a network for faith formation among the young.

MENTORS IN SCRIPTURE

While the contemporary focus on mentoring may have been influenced by broader developments in management theory and education, the practice of older and more experienced figures guiding and instructing younger people is found throughout the Bible. Intentional mentoring relationships are also reflected in relationships between Moses and Joshua, Elijah and Elisha, Jesus and his disciples, and Paul and Timothy.

The biblical treatment of "elders" reflects the assumption that older members of the community will provide guidance and leadership to the young. While elders refers to a distinct age span, the Bible also sees a body of elders, chosen for their wisdom and experience, as responsible for leading God's people. In the Old Testament, God instructs Moses to tell the elders of Israel about his promise to deliver the Israelites from Egypt (Exod 3:16–21), and, later in his ministry, gives seventy elders a share of his authority to lead the people (Num 11:16–25). In the New Testament, elders are appointed to help lead the early church, a practice particularly reflected in Acts (14:23; 15:23; 20:17) and in the Pastoral Epistles (1 Tim 4:14; 5:17; Titus 1:5).[5]

The association between age and wisdom is also reflected in the book of Proverbs, which includes aphorisms directed from an elder to a youth. Traditionally associated with Solomon, the elder shares the wisdom gained by experience and observation, and passes it on to the next generation.

In Proverbs 4, the elder (or father) addresses the reader as "children," and calls for attention to wisdom, the "beautiful crown" that is bestowed on those who heed her voice (4:9). While much of Proverbs offers wisdom for all in the community, many of its verses specifically address youth. Hence, wisdom is given about work (6:6–11), marriage (5:15–19; 31), and righteous living (3:27–35). In the intergenerational communities of ancient

---

5. Elders are also mentioned in James (5:15) and 1 Peter (5:1, 5). The author of 2 John and 3 John describes himself as "the elder" (2 John 1; 3 John 1),while Revelation depicts twenty-four elders—who represent all who follow Christ—in the heavenly throne room (Rev 4:4, 10; 5:8).

Israel, it was common for the elders—both the leaders of the community and the older generation—to mentor the young, passing on wisdom for living.[6]

The biblical stress on elders is balanced by the way in which the voices of the young often speak truth or model godliness, but it is significant that it is often elders who recognize their voices. While Samuel receives the prophetic word from God, it is the elder Eli who recognizes it (1 Sam 3:1–9). While the twelve-year-old Jesus confounds the religious leaders with his wisdom, Mary and Joseph continue to guide Jesus as his parents (Luke 2:41–51). While Paul appoints Timothy as leader of the church in Ephesus (1 Tim 1:3–4; 4:6–10), Paul also appoints elders who need Timothy's support (1 Tim 5:17–22).

Alongside the encouragement of the young to look to elders, and of elders to relate to the young, the Bible also presents examples of mentoring in action through its exploration of key biblical figures. While these examples are not quite the same as formal mentoring relationships today,[7] they show figures of maturity encouraging and equipping those who are younger to trust and to follow God

An early biblical example is the relationship between Moses and Joshua. Moses, the prophet and messenger of God, is appointed as leader of Israel and given the task of leading Israel out of Egypt (Exod 3:1–12), but it is Joshua who later leads Israel into the Promised Land.

Joshua first appears as a military leader during the Exodus (Exod 17), and later accompanies Moses to Sinai (24:12–18). Joshua is described as Moses' "assistant," and has the privilege of witnessing God's glory in the giving of the law. When Moses later encounters the Lord in the "tent of meeting," Joshua is there too, lingering behind as Moses leaves (Exod 33:11). Joshua later becomes Moses' successor, and takes the reigns of leadership as Israel conquers Canaan and sees the fulfillment of God's promises to Moses. As well as encountering God's presence alongside Moses, we can presume that Joshua learned leadership through spending time with Moses and observing his role. Having been mentored by Moses, Joshua became a great leader.

---

6. On intergenerational relationships in the Bible, see Allen and Ross, *Intergenerational Christian Formation*, 77–84.

7. Unlike formal mentoring relationships today, for example, mentoring relationships in the Bible typically took place when the mentee worked or lived alongside the mentor, with guidance coming "on the road."

A similar kind of relationship is found between the prophets Elijah and Elisha. Elijah is instructed by God to appoint Elisha as his successor, and so Elijah calls him from relative obscurity and declares that he has been chosen by God (1 Kgs 19:19–21). The narrative continues to focus on Elijah's ministry until 2 Kings 2, when Elijah "passes the mantle" of prophetic authority to Elisha. Although the presence of Elisha prior to his succession is not mentioned, the text assumes that Elisha had been with Elijah since his anointing. Second Kings 2, for example, begins with the note that "Elijah and Elisha were on their way from Gilgal" (2:1).

The companionship of Elisha with the great Elijah prepares the way for his succession. Elisha receives a double share of the prophetic Spirit, doing even greater miracles than his mentor. Elijah has passed on his wisdom and gifts to Elisha, who continues the prophetic work among God's people.

In the New Testament, Jesus also acts as a mentor—a model and a guide—to his disciples.[8] Discipleship can be seen as an ancient form of mentoring, where a rabbi taught and instructed his students in the life of faith.[9] The disciples spend time with Jesus, accompany him during ministry in Galilee and follow him to Jerusalem. They observe his miracles, hear his teaching, ask questions, and receive further insight into Jesus' life and ministry. As Smither points out, such mentoring was communal, rather than one to one, and reflected the group context of the ancient world.[10]

Intriguingly, the risen Jesus mentors his disciples after his resurrection, unveiling their eyes and their hearts to the reality before them (Luke 24:13–27). Jesus also promises the Spirit, who comes as "another Advocate," a comforter and encourager to help people in the life of faith (John 14:15–31). While mentoring is probably a term best confined to human relationships, the New Testament teaching on the Spirit is a reminder of the spiritual dimension of God's leading.

A final example of mentoring is found in the relationship between Paul and his protégé Timothy. Timothy is first mentioned in Acts (16:1–5), where Paul invites him to be a companion for his missionary journeys.

---

8. In our previous chapter, we suggested that the relationship might also be described in terms of friendship, since the text itself suggests that was a term Jesus had adopted. While being their friend, however, Jesus remained the Lord of his disciples and their rabbi and teacher.

9. For the relationship between mentoring and discipleship, as well as helpful discussion of mentoring in the New Testament, see Smither, *Augustine as Mentor*, 1–23.

10. Ibid., 13–14. Smither also argues that group mentoring was more effective in establishing the church as a community of disciples.

As the son of a Gentile father and a Jewish mother, Paul has Timothy circumcised, meaning that Timothy could reach Jews as well as Gentiles—a key strategy in the Pauline mission (16:3). Timothy accompanies Paul on his journeys, no doubt learning alongside Paul as they traveled together (17:14–15).

In his letters, Paul describes Timothy as a "beloved and faithful child in the Lord" (1 Cor 4:16–17 cf. Phil 2:22), and entrusts him with the difficult task of challenging and encouraging churches (1 Cor 4:17; 1 Thess 3:12). The Pastoral Epistles also provide us with Paul's unique second-person engagement with Timothy.[11] Now a church leader, Paul continues to mentor Timothy, offering advice and encouragement. Timothy should remain faithful, keeping close to God while maintaining true doctrine (1 Tim 4:6–10). Timothy should also seek to mentor others, both as an example (4:11–12) and as a teacher (4:12–16). Although young, Timothy is a example of God's power at work.

The Bible, then, depicts informal mentoring taking place as those who are mature provide models of faith and wisdom for the young. As well as this, it also provides examples of more intentional mentoring.

Mentoring has also played a key role throughout Christian history.[12] Saint Augustine was mentored by older Christian men, and also became a mentor to others through his writings, teaching, and relationships.[13] In the medieval era, Catherine of Sienna, a fourteenth-century theologian and nun, mentored others through letters of spiritual direction, while in the twentieth-century context of the Confessing Church, Dietrich Bonhoeffer was an influential mentor in the lives of those who knew him.[14]

MENTORING AND FAITH

While mentoring has always been part of human community, there is a lack of adult mentors in today's society. This is due, in part at least, to the way in

---

11. Some biblical scholars argue that the Pastoral Epistles were written by a later writer (in this view, the letters are pseudonymous), but even if post-Pauline, 1 Timothy presents a picture of the mentoring relationship between Paul and Timothy. Stott argues for the Pauline authorship of 1 Timothy and, throughout his commentary, draws attention to the relationship between Paul and his protégé (*Message of 1 Timothy*).

12. For brief surveys of mentoring within Christian history, see Williams, *Potter's Rib*, 189–263; and Lewis, *Mentoring Matters*, 39–67.

13. Smither, *Augustine as Mentor*.

14. For these two examples, see Williams, *Potter's Rib*, 209–17, 237–50.

which youth and adults are segregated in life. Young people have less and less opportunity to relate to adults outside the family, and the church has often supported such segregation instead of challenging it.[15] Adults can also feel that they have little to offer young people, particularly when the younger generation can access information and resources far more easily than in the past.

Mentors, however, remain crucially important for young people. Mentors help young people in their development and play a key role in modeling and passing on the beliefs or values of a community.

The importance of mentors for the development of young people is well established in studies of youth development. Mentors can prevent young people from engaging in harmful or at-risk behavior, such as drug use.[16] In one study of almost one thousand children and young teenagers, those who had a mentor were also less likely to misbehave in class.[17]

Mentors also positively encourage young people's development. One review of the literature found that the presence and number of caring adults in adolescents' lives is the most important factor for positive youth development.[18] Young people who experience poverty and family disruption are more likely to thrive if they have at least one adult who provided consistent emotional support.[19] Similarly, a young person is likely to mirror the behavior of their adult mentor.[20] Having a mentor means that young people will do better at school, and are more likely to build good and positive relationships.

The value of mentors for young people has led to the rise of government and volunteer programs that seek to provide mentors for at-risk young people. While many young people will naturally form mentoring relationships, those "at risk" may struggle to do so, and so government programs seek to capitalize on the value of mentors for all youth. In one study of such programs, scholars argued that they were valuable and effective, but pointed to the priority for mentors to establish good and positive relationships with the mentees.[21]

---

15. So Allen and Ross, *Intergenerational Christian Formation*, 29–46. For a helpful discussion on how to restore relationships between the generations, see also Gardner, *Mend the Gap*.

16. See Sipe, "Mentoring Programs for Adolescents," 252.

17. Centre for Addiction and Mental Health, "Youth Mentoring."

18. Bowers, *Promoting Positive Youth Development*, 110.

19. Greenberger et al., "Role of 'Very Important' Nonparental Adults," 322.

20. Ibid., 321–43.

21. DeBois et al., "How Effective Are Mentoring Programs for Youth?"

But why is it that mentors are so important? Unlike parents, mentors provide an outside voice that can affirm and encourage a young person. Most parents will naturally love their child and invest time and energy in helping them grow. A mentor, however, chooses to do so, and this affirmation of the young person's value means that they are likely to grow through such relationships. While engaging with friends and a peer group helps shape a young person's identity, a mentor provides a more experienced voice that can affirm and encourage the young person.

Young people also learn by modeling their behavior on those around them, including the adults that they know. As Allen and Ross argue, religious socialization requires relationships between young people and adults. It is as young people are integrated into a religious community, and actively develop relationships within it, that they are "socialized" into Christian faith.[22]

The importance of a mentor was crucial to Adrian's faith as a teenager. At aged fourteen, he had great parents but thought they were "naff" and could not see life the way they did. But even if he did not appreciate their support, Adrian still longed for adult affirmation. Being in a youth group with two adult leaders, Tim and Rose, provided other adult voices in his life. While they could not replace his parents, Tim and Rose were able to offer Adrian a supportive voice as he grew in faith while also being examples of Christian life.

Mentoring, then, can be a significant influence on the life of faith, and those young people who are mentored are far more likely to remain within the church. In one recent study of millennials raised in the church, those who had remained active in church after secondary school were twice as likely to have a close personal friendship with an adult within the church.[23] Those who had a more formal relationship with an adult mentor other than the pastor were also more likely to stay part of the church.[24]

Research carried out among Methodists in Britain revealed that young people desired adult affirmation in their faith journey. Such adults act as cheerleaders, guides, and mentors, and demonstrate what a future faith

---

22. Allen and Ross, *Intergenerational Christian Formation*, 121–38. See also the description of the range of ways in which adults teach faith to young people in Smith and Denton, *Soul Searching*, 286.

23. Barna Group, "5 Reasons." 59 percent of those who stayed active in church report such a friendship versus 31 percent among those who are no longer active.

24. As the research report notes, correlation is not the same as causation, but it is nonetheless striking that the majority of those who left the church failed to have any significant relationship with a Christian adult (outside a parent), including a mentoring relationship.

might look like. Such mentors are open to conversation and discussion with young people, and are a steady presence, a sign of God's grace within the community. This becomes even more important for young people who do not have Christian parents who can model faith to them.

As well as helping Christians remain in the church, mentors can help young people live out their faith. First-year college students who experienced natural Christian mentoring were more willing to serve others than those who had not had such an experience. Often, their mentoring began in their mid-teen years, and their connection to the Christian community was important to their success and development. Natural mentoring relationships during the mid-teen years have an impact on how committed adolescents remain to church and to those long-term interpersonal relationships that are beneficial for both them and others.[25]

Teenagers need to interact with people of all ages in the church. Those in their twenties can be guides for their transition into work or further education, while those closer to their parents' age can show them an example of faith for the future. The elders in the church can offer them the wisdom of experience and a link to the older generation.

MODELING FAITH WITH YOUNG PEOPLE

While God is the one who nurtures and gives life to those in faith, church leaders, parents, and youth leaders are called by God to encourage all within the church, including young people, to grow in faith. Mentoring, whether formal or informal, is one way in which this takes place, and the research suggests that it plays a greater role than some might expect. But how exactly can the church nurture the mentors in its midst?

Firstly, the church needs to work harder at creating contexts for informal mentoring opportunities. Informal mentoring can take place when a young person observes the faith or love of an older Christian, and, seeing it, is inspired to deepen their own faith or love. Or it can take place when an older Christian takes time to get to know a younger Christian, chatting to them about their life, the challenges they face, or the hopes that they have. The significance of such informal mentoring is often underrated, but it is through seeing living faith among elders that the young learn what it is to be mature in Christ.[26]

25. Lanker and Issler, "Relationship," 104.

26. See DeVries description of the church as the "extended Christian family," with

Creating such informal mentoring opportunities begins with finding ways of young and old to mix together within the family of faith, whether in the church building, at home over a meal, or at social or sports events. If the church is a family, then the role of adults in raising youth should not be confined to parents or to youth workers but is part of what all within the church are called to do. Religious socialization takes place when the older and younger mix together, with those who are mature modeling and showing the path of faith to those who are young.[27]

Informal mentoring also place when younger Christians hear the testimonies of older or more mature Christians. Often, adolescents have little idea of the issues of faith that older people face, or the way in which faith has sustained them through difficult times. Finding times for such sharing to take place can be transformative. It can help faith come alive. The church should seek out opportunities for such storytelling, knowing the impact it can have on all.

An informal mentoring environment also provides a perfect environment for what are called "natural mentoring" relationships.[28] Natural mentoring refers to a mentoring relationship that emerges organically over a number of years, typically involving a commitment by the mentor to meet with and support the mentee. Such a relationship usually begins when the mentee is in their early adolescence, and is somewhere between an informal and a formal relationship. They are informal inasmuch as they emerge organically and without a program, but they are formal in that they involve intentionality. However described, such relationships are a joy to witness, and sharing examples of such relationships can be a good way to nurture the potential of future mentors.

A second way in which the church can nurture mentors is through creating opportunities for formal mentoring relationships between adults and youth. Formal mentoring can embrace a variety of forms, such as discipling, coaching, and spiritual direction.[29] In each case, a formal mentoring

---

adults providing examples and models of Christian maturity to teenagers (DeVries, *Family-Based Youth Ministry*, 82–95). See also Powell and Clark, *Sticky Faith*, 93–122, who describe the importance of adults in churches taking an interest in the lives of teenagers and young adults.

27. Allen and Ross, *Intergenerational Christian Formation*, 121–38 .

28. On the importance of such relationships, see Lanker, "Life-Long Guides"; Lanker, "Family of Faith"; and Lanker and Issler, "Relationship."

29. Stanley and Clinton, in *Connecting*, describe these three types as forms of "intensive mentoring."

relationship is structured and intentional, requiring commitment and time on both sides. Often it will be the youth worker who takes on the role of a mentor to youth, perhaps meeting a young person over Bible study, or praying together. In all such relationships, it is important that the mentor and the mentee have a natural affinity or warmth with each another.

One form of mentoring relationship that can helpfully be developed within the church is the coach within a mission situation. While a formal mentoring relationship, it will tend to be limited to the duration of the mission trip or event—but, while it lasts, such a relationship can build up the young person and help them to grow in faith as they serve God in mission.

Mentoring can also take place with a group of young people, and such group mentoring was characteristic of Jesus' ministry. While mentoring may be difficult in larger groups, a mentor can take the time to model and pass on wisdom to a smaller group of two or three.

Finally, we should note the importance of what some authors call "reverse mentoring," where those who are mature in years learn from the wisdom of the young.[30] Adults need the enthusiasm of young people and their new experiences with God to keep their faith alive and fresh.[31] Youth can often provide such energy, and also practical skills and wisdom for relating the gospel to life's challenges today. One area where reverse mentoring can take place is around the challenges and possibilities of engaging in culture. While older Christians may be tempted to retreat from cultural engagement, teenagers are often the quickest to see the ways in which the gospel can speak to culture, either as challenge or encouragement. The enthusiasm and willingness to risk all for faith that many young people have can also be contagious, both for mentors and for others members of a Christian community.

CONCLUSION

Mentors can be a massive influence on the lives of young people. They can speak truth with love into the lives of others, see the potential of young people when others do not, and take the time to encourage and build them up into the image of Christ.

Mentoring, then, is a key network for faith formation. The church should seek to find and nurture spaces for such relationships to develop

---

30. Creps, *Reverse Mentoring*.

31. The anthropologist Roy Rappaport argues that it was young person's encounters with God that kept the church's faith fresh (*Ritual and Religion*, 396).

informally, while also providing short-term opportunities for formal mentoring to occur. In both cases, the quality of relationship between the mentor and the mentee is key. When there is mutual respect and affection, then mentoring can be a powerful and incredibly significant network that builds up the faith of the younger and emerging generations.

Like all such networks, mentoring relationships work best when embedded in a cluster of other relationships. When they are, they can powerfully help teenagers grow in their faith.

PUTTING IT INTO PRACTICE

- If you are a youth worker, encourage parents to attend or help out at youth events throughout the year. Mentors are often found among parents, especially when parents take the time to know their children's friends.

- Encourage young people to seek out adult mentors within the church, and adults to build up informal friendships with young people! Adults who take the time to seek out and speak to a young person regularly can have a huge impact on their lives.

- When planning for a mission trip (see chapter 9), consider setting up a mentoring relationship between some of the adult helpers and the youth. You do not need to label this as mentoring, but such a relationship can be an opportunity for the more mature to pass on wisdom to the younger, while also building them up in faith and love.

FURTHER READING

Egeler, Daniel. *Mentoring Millennials: Shaping the Next Generation*. Colorado Springs, CO: NavPress, 2003.

While drawing on the models of mentoring developed by Stanley and Clinton, Egeler focuses on the challenges and opportunities of mentoring the millennial generation.

Johnson, W. Brad, and Charles R. Ridley. *The Elements of Mentoring*. Rev. ed. London: Palgrave Macmillan, 2004.

Although not a theological work, this helpful book gives a host of good tips for (formal) mentors.

Stanley, Paul D., and J. Robert Clinton. *Connecting: The Mentoring Relationships You Need to Succeed in Life*. Colorado Springs, CO: NavPress, 1992.

Stanley and Clinton offer a broad approach to mentoring that shows the range of ways in which Christians can shape the lives of others.

7

Small Groups
Community Faith

By our willingness to join and participate in small groups we signal our desire to walk with others on the road to transformation.

Roger Walton[1]

INTRODUCTION

While small groups were rare in much of twentieth-century church life,[2] you would be hard pressed today to find a church without them. A range of church leaders advocate such groups as a key means of discipleship development,[3] and a multitude of books are available to help small groups in the task. Small groups also play a vital role in youth ministry, with the community they generate and the accountability they offer providing a key place for young people to grow in faith. Despite some critics,[4] small groups

1. Walton, *Disciples Together*, 151.

2. While we will argue that small groups have featured throughout Christian history, they were not part of many churches for much of the twentieth century. That changed in the 1960s and 70s, when small groups became more and more prominent within the life of all churches. For a historical and sociological account of the growth of small groups in America, see Wuthnow, *Sharing the Journey*.

3. For the value of small groups within church life, see Cameron, *Resourcing Mission*, 24–37; Walton, *Disciples Together*, 69–84.

4. For one illustrative example, see Jones, "Why Churches Should Euthanize Small Groups."

are likely here to stay—and so they should, given their impact on the lives of those who attend them.

Inviting friends on Facebook to share stories of the impact that a small group had on their own teenage lives, I (Steve) received numerous accounts, all of which movingly pointed to their impact:[5]

> Being involved in a youth group and youth ministry in my teen years was life changing. I saw peers differently than I did in school; I saw their vulnerabilities like I hadn't before. I experienced, for the first time, the gift of the Holy Spirit in my life during a youth group gathering. These experiences, as well as being involved in my church, set me on the path to keep God in my life.

> The youth group were encouraged to join in with mission activities and I can still picture myself sharing my faith in street dramas. It taught me that evangelism was important and that all of us had responsibility for sharing our faith.

> The discipleship, friendship, guidance, and most of all love I had received from the youth leaders at the time couldn't have come at a better time in my life. . . . It was so good just being part of group of people who supported, guided, and were a positive influence in my life.

While a small group can be defined in a number of different ways, we will be using the term to refer to groups of three to twelve that seek to nurture and encourage participants in their Christian life. Youth groups often take a small group format, and such small groups help young people deepen their faith. Small groups can also have a variety of purposes, including Bible study, accountability, and spiritual support, but all have has an intentionally formative dimension.[6]

In this chapter, we argue for the importance of small groups as a network for faith formation that helps young people to grow in their faith. We begin by looking at the precedents for small groups within the early church,

---

5. While these responses are anecdotal and self-selecting, they illustrate what the broader research reveals. The quotes come from adults who were in faith based groups as teenagers; the first in the US, the second in England, and the third in the Pacific Islands.

6. Such groups differ, then, from small groups that have a purely social function. While these are not the focus of this chapter, they too can have an important role. Within a church context, they allow young people to get to know one another more deeply, and, whether peer group or intergenerational, they allow space for relationships to be built and to be nurtured.

noting that house churches had three key characteristics that small groups emulate today: spiritual intimacy, mutual support, and mutual accountability. Small groups have also existed throughout history, with many historical models inspiring developments in the church today. We next focus on the way in which small groups shape the life and the faith of young people, particularly in providing a kind of support not readily available in larger groups. Finally, we suggest two ways in which church leaders can encourage and nurture small group ministry among their youth.

SMALL GROUPS IN SCRIPTURE

The Old Testament gives examples of the worship of God taking place in the small group of a household,[7] and the emphasis on formation in community that the Old Testament depicts offers principles that can be helpful for small group ministry today.[8] Most advocates of small group ministry, however, rightly look to the New Testament house church as a closer precedent for small group ministry today.[9] Like today's small groups, house churches embodied key values and practices that enabled God's people to flourish. In particular, house churches provided a sphere of intimacy, a place of mutual support, and a community of accountability.

The sphere of intimacy found within small groups is reflected throughout the New Testament. As we noted in our discussion of the church, early Christians treated one another as members of a family, and particularly as siblings—one of the strongest relational bonds of the ancient world.[10] Christians addressed each other as brothers and sisters (Rom 1:13; Heb 3:1; Jas 1:2),[11] greeted one another with a holy kiss (2 Cor 13:12), and treated

7. The Old Testament household included not just the (nuclear) family, but a wider circle of associates and relations that all sat under a patriarchal "head." An Israelite household, then, was in some respects a small group in which worship and formation took place—though, of course, this is quite different from small groups today!

8. See, for example, Icenogle's application of the Ten Commandments to small group ministry (*Biblical Foundations*, 46–66).

9. See, for example, Atkinson and Comiskey, "'Lessons from the Early House Church." The authors conclude that the house church can act as a "helpful prototype" for cell groups today, though they also acknowledge that this should be done with caution (85–86).

10. As Hellerman argues in *When the Church Was a Family*, in the biblical world a brother or sister was closer than a spouse.

11. In Greek, the address is typically "brothers" (*adelphoi*), though the NRSV

each other with love and care. As those adopted by God as their Father, Christians saw themselves as called to show radical love to others within the church (1 John 3:1, 11–18).

The meeting places of early Christians were primarily households and this nurtured a sense of intimacy within the church.[12] Since Christians were family to one another, the unity found in Christ undercut social divisions and judgements (Gal 3:28). Hence, Paul opposed those in Corinth who distributed the Communion meal in such a way as to reflect or reinforce divisions of rich and poor (1 Cor 11:20–22).[13] For Paul, the intimacy that God's grace encouraged within the church meant that such division was anathema, a stain on the community.

House churches also provided natural places of mutual support. Since the numbers within the community would be limited by space,[14] those who attended church would find themselves in an intergenerational and socially diverse community where each would know the other, and where each would offer support. Such support would be emotional as well as practical, spiritual as well as physical.

The New Testament teaching on giving and generosity illustrates the support found within first-century churches. While it supports "almsgiving," setting aside money for the poor within the wider community (Matt 6:1–4), the New Testament particularly highlights the obligations of Christians to offer financial help to other Christians suffering hardship (2 Cor 8:1–15). Paul encouraged Gentile Christians to assist their Jewish brethren suffering poverty and hardship (Rom 15:30–31; 2 Cor 9), and James called Christians to show evidence of their faith through caring for the poor and needy in their community (Jas 2:14–17).

House churches also provided a place of accountability. Since each member would know the other, each was called to help "bear one another's burdens" (Gal 2:20) and encourage one another in the life of faith (Heb 3:13). Accountability would include watching that others do not "wander

---

translation "brothers and sisters" acknowledges that the term is inclusive of both genders.

12. Atkinson and Comiskey, "Lessons from the Early House Church," 82–83.

13. For a description of the likely situation at Corinth, see Thiselton, *1 Corinthians*, 181–82.

14. Given the different types of houses and buildings in the ancient world, it is difficult to estimate the amount of people within a house church. After a careful discussion, Osiek and Bach note that "Many Christians assemblies were certainly much smaller than 40; others could have been significantly larger" (*Families in the New Testament World*, 203).

from the faith" (Jas 5:19), but doing so with love and gentleness (Gal 6:1). It would also include encouraging others to live out their faith.

At times, accountability would also mean disassociating from those who would tear apart the community through false teaching. While a feature of the letters of Paul (Gal 1:6–9), such an occasion is also addressed by the elder of 2 John. Facing a situation where false teachings who had left the church were seeking to draw others into their sphere, the elder instructed members of the church to avoid hosting or supporting the false teacher (2 John 10–11). Accountability in this context meant ensuring that other members of the community would be protected from erroneous views of God.

Household churches, then, provided a sphere of intimacy, a place of support, and a community of accountability, and it is precisely these three values that small groups in the contemporary world value and seek to reflect. Such values can and should influence Christian thinking on small groups. We should also note, however, that the New Testament house churches also differed from contemporary small groups—primarily in including all the elements of church found in services today.[15] Small groups are not the same as first-century house churches, even if they have a lot to learn from them.

As well as drawing inspiration from the New Testament, today's small groups can also look back to the many examples of small groups that have emerged in Christian history.[16] These have included the small groups set up by St. Francis to promote evangelistic renewal within the church,[17] the *collegia* of the Pietist movement of the seventeenth and eighteenth centuries, and the classes and bands associated with the Methodist revival of the eighteenth century.

The contemporary interest in small groups emerged in the 1960s, when, in response to the loss of community within wider society, churches began to include small groups within their repertoire of offerings.[18] Given their focus on community, such small groups often prioritize intimacy over

15. An exception to this point might be the cell church movement, which does see each "cell" or small group as church.

16. For the history of small groups in the post-Reformation era, see Bunton, "300 Years of Small Groups." For the history of the small group movement in the twentieth and twenty-first centuries, see Walton, *Disciples Together*, 85–107.

17. Thompson, *St. Francis of Assisi*.

18. For the history, see Wuthnow, *Sharing the Journey*; and Walton, *Disciples Together*, 85–107.

challenge,[19] but a range of alternative small groups have emerged today and they are likely to feature in churches for the foreseeable future.

SMALL GROUPS AND FAITH

Young people and emerging adults frequently meet together in small groups, and working in small groups is a part of the educational sector as well as work life today. In a highly individualistic culture that distrusts institutions and authority, small groups provide emotional support and a vision beyond individualism.[20] Small groups are also a strong feature of church and youth ministry today, and the evidence shows that they help young people—and, indeed, all within the church—to retain and strengthen their faith.

Evidence for the link between small groups and faith is found in a number of studies. One study of large congregations, for instance, found that those involved in small groups were far more likely to be committed to the church, and the researchers noted that the finding was true for smaller congregations as well. As the study noted, "Small group members report a greater sense of belonging, attend services more frequently, and contribute a higher percentage of their income to their congregation."[21] A UMC report on vital congregations, based on a survey of over 32,000 congregations, also identified "small groups and programs" as one of the four key areas that fuel vitality.[22] Resources on church growth also prioritize the role of small group ministry.[23]

Why is it, then, that small groups are so important for faith, and particularly for helping to develop the faith of young people and emerging adults? Small groups are vital because they provide in today's context the

19. Wuthnow, "Small Groups."

20. Bauman, *Liquid Times*, 5–17.

21. Dougherty and Whitehead, "Place to Belong," 107. For the correlation of small group involvement with congregational participation, see also Donahue and Gowler, "Small Groups," 126; and Walton, *Disciples Together*, 115.

22. See United Methodist Church, "Vital Congregations." The other three practices are: worship services with mixed traditional and contemporary styles and relevant sermons, pastors who work hard on mentorship and cultivation of the laity, and an emphasis on effective lay leadership. These four practices are consistent regardless of church size, predominant ethnicity, and jurisdiction.

23. See, for example, the way in which Schnase links "intentional faith development," one of the "five practices of fruitful congregations," with "learning in community," which often takes place through different kinds of small groups (*Five Practices*, 59–78).

key values found in our study of New Testament house churches: a sphere of intimacy, a place of mutual support, and a place of accountability. For young people in particular, each of these values is important for helping faith to develop and to grow.

The way in which small groups provide a sphere of intimacy for young people has been widely attested in the literature. Developmentally, finding such spheres—places where people know your name, acknowledge your gifts, and treasure your contributions—is key for teenagers. Intimacy involves a sense of belonging to a group, and it is such belonging that small groups can help to develop.

Such a sphere of intimacy is particularly important when young people find themselves disaffiliated from the institutional church. Being connected with a small group means that young people are more likely to keep the faith even if they find Sunday services difficult. It provides a community where they know others well, and allows them a positive connection to the church through the relationships they build.

Small groups are also important because, like the early house churches, they provide a place of mutual support. Such support will show itself in different ways, and can be spiritual, emotional, and practical. The experience of taking part in a small group will strengthen the threads of relationship between participants, and will encourage a community where each looks after the other. Such support shows young people that the church cares, and gives people a sense of God's care through human actions.

Small groups also support young people as they develop a sense of faith, a task that is harder than ever in an increasingly secularized and post-Christian society. While wider society may offer criticism and negativity about Christian faith to young people, the existence of a small group of other Christians who are seeking to live and speak of faith gives individuals more confidence in the faith for themselves.

Finally, small groups provide a place of accountability. As one study shows, there is a correlation between those who commit to a small group and those who grow deeper in their commitment to God.[24] Small groups provide a place to explore faith and to challenge one another to grow more deeply into faith.[25] For young people in particular, small groups are a place

24. Knabb, "Cord of Three Strands," 354. Knabb points out that the converse is true too; those who avoid attachments to others were also reticent in their attachment to God. Knabb's study shows that our connection with others is also, then, deeply linked to our connection to God.

25. Donahue and Gowler note that small group members report an "enhanced

to learn the life of faith, with participation in the group allowing transformational learning about faith.[26] Taking part in such small groups is one way in which individual identity is shaped during adolescence, and such an influence enhances adherence to religious norms and behaviors of the group.[27] In short, small groups reinforce and nurture faith commitments.[28]

While accountability has a powerful impact on the lives of those in small groups, we should also note that this is one area of small group ministry that is often weak. Wuthnow's study of small groups, for instance, identified a tendency of small groups to emphasize emotional support over the challenge and call of discipleship.[29] A study of small groups in the North East of England also found that they tended to stress personal support and inward spirituality over missional engagement or discerning God's activity in the world.[30] Accountability is one reason for the effectiveness of small groups, but such groups can neglect this dimension, offering support and companionship without the call to discipleship that is always needed in Christian faith formation.[31]

NURTURING FAITH IN COMMUNITY

Since small groups have been recognized as so important for churches, how exactly should churches encourage their development? How, in particular, can churches envision the role of small groups in developing the faith of young people?

Firstly, church leaders should develop small groups to stretch and help the faith of young people. Youth workers, of course, typically encourage such groups, and working with them is often a natural part of their role, whether as Sunday school meetings, Bible studies, or evening events. The expertise of youth pastors in discipling youth in such groups is often something from which others in the church can learn. Nonetheless, churches

---

spiritual life" ("Small Groups," 125).

26. See Shepherd, *Faith Generation*, 99–116.

27. Regnerus, *Forbidden Fruit*, 197

28. Dougherty and Whitehead, "Place to Belong", 107–9.

29. Wuthnow, *Sharing the Journey*.

30. Walton, "Disciples Together."

31. See also Withrow, "Disciples for the Future," which offers suggestions to prevent small groups from becoming overly privatized.

can always be reminded that such spaces offer a unique opportunity to help young people inhabit the faith for themselves.

Church leaders and workers need to be intentional in setting up small groups to build and nurture faith.[32] Creating a space for young people to gather is not the same as creating a space for faith formation. While both sorts of group groups can play a role in helping young people to belong, the church needs to focus on ways in which the small groups provides a context for young people to learn the faith.[33] Such small groups can provide a place for young people to explore faith in all its complexity, and also to develop the capacity to speak of faith. Learning the language of faith is critical to faith formation because it allows youth—and all within the church—to inhabit it more deeply.[34]

A second way of supporting the role of small groups is to integrate them into the wider ministry and life of the church. If the people of God includes those of every generation, and if the service of Word and Sacrament is central to the formation of young people, then the small group should be seen as an activity alongside the main worship of God's people. Small groups are not a replacement for church, or a "young people's church" in themselves, but rather form part of the church that gathers together in worship.[35] By linking small groups to the larger church, leaders and youth workers can signal to the young people that they too belong to the church, while also highlighting the importance of being shaped by the worship of the church through Word and Sacrament.[36]

There are a range of ways to promote relationships and links between small groups and the wider church. One possibility would be to create intergenerational small groups, so that young and old meet together to learn and worship.[37] Another possibility would be to ensure that young people are engaging with similar content to others in the church. Instead of having a separate curriculum for youth, young and old could independently explore similar topics or texts. However a church engages, it is important

32. On this point, see Shepherd, *Faith Generation*, 127.

33. On the need for church leaders to teach the faith, see Smith and Denton, *Soul Searching*, 267–68. "Teaching" in this context refers to all the formal and informal ways in which knowledge and experience is communicated from one to another.

34. Smith and Denton, *Soul Searching*, 268.

35. Our position differs from that of Wijnen and Barnard, who argues that small groups can serve as church for young people ("Connected to the Wellspring").

36. See our earlier discussion in chapter 3.

37. Allen and Ross, *Intergenerational Faith Formation*, 239–47.

to consider the different ways in which small groups of young people find ways to belong, find support, and be kept accountable to the wider church.

CONCLUSION

Small groups are a key context in which young people develop faith. It is in small groups that young people as well as adults can find a sense of community and feel that they really belong. Small groups also provide support for young people, including a space that can sustain them as they explore difficult issues of faith. And small groups can places of accountability and challenge, encouraging young people to live out their faith.

In short, small groups provide a network for faith formation, a way in which churches can help young people to develop their faith. While they are not the whole answer to growing faith, they can be a particularly important place for adolescents within the church.

PUTTING IT INTO PRACTICE

- Explore how small groups are currently functioning among the young people in your church. To what extent do they currently help young people develop faith?

- Church history offers a range of examples of small groups renewing and transforming the church. The eighteenth-century evangelical revival, for example, relied on the classes and bands set up by John Wesley. Within your church or small group, take the time to explore a historical small group model. What can it teach the church today?

- How are youth groups within your church linked into the rest of the church's ministry? Explore the relationships between the content, format, or style of youth groups and the rest of the church; where are the links and continuities between them? How much does the wider church know about what takes place in the youth groups?

FURTHER READING

Frazee, Randy. *The Connecting Church: Beyond Small Groups to Authentic Community*. Grand Rapids: Zondervan, 2001.

Critiquing some models of small group ministry, Frazee develops an intentional approach to building community within the church that also shapes the development of small groups.

Hellerman, Joseph H. *When the Church Was a Family: Recapturing Jesus' Vision for Authentic Christian Community*. Nashville: B&H, 2009.

Hellerman explores how the depiction of the church as family in the NT challenges our understanding of what it means to be a community today.

Shepherd, Nick. *Faith Generation: Retaining Young People and Growing the Church*. London: SPCK, 2016.

Drawing on detailed research, Shepherd argues for the importance of youth ministry and explores how youth workers and church leaders can help young people grow in faith today.

8

Events and Gatherings
Deepening Faith

Many youth will point to a retreat experience as the moment in their spiritual journey when they were first able (or best able) to make a commitment to God.

Kenda Creasy Dean and Ron Foster[1]

INTRODUCTION

Eleven-year-old Becky had never been very keen on camps or festivals. Apart from an awful school trip, where she spent three miserable days at a cold and wet campsite, she had not spent more than a night away from home. When her youth worker invited teens in the church to attend a Christian summer camp, he was not surprised that Becky counted herself out. Her friends were excited about the event, but Becky explained that it was not her kind of thing.

Her youth worker, however, encouraged Becky to consider coming, with her parents suggesting it might be better than she feared. As summer approached, Becky took a risk and joined eighty other campers at a youth center a couple of hours from home. With activities and games during the morning, and excursions to the surrounding countryside each afternoon, the camp was a great deal of fun. It was also a time of deepening faith. Each

---

1. Dean and Foster, *Godbearing Life*, 190.

day began with prayer and Bible study, and the evenings included a time of sung worship and testimony around the campfire.

When she returned home from the event, Becky seemed transformed. She spoke about times of encountering God over discussions at night, and how she had never realized that Jesus was quite so incredible. Although the impact of the event gradually faded, Becky looked back to it as deeply formative to her faith and the beginning of her annual trip to summer camp.

Camps, festivals,[2] and pilgrimages can all play a significant role within youth ministry. They each involve traveling to a different place and engaging with a different kind of community, and each includes a focus—at least in Christian settings—on encountering God.

In this chapter, we focus on the significance of events and gatherings for the faith formation of young people. We begin by exploring Scripture, describing the important festivals and pilgrimages of the Old Testament and their displacement in the New. We also look at the practice of pilgrimage throughout history, and the more recent development of camps and Christian festivals. We next explore the sociological impact that events and gatherings can have on young people. Such occasions offer an experience of deep community, deep worship, and transformative learning. Finally, we point to ways in which church leaders, youth pastors, and parents can build on the impact of such occasions, including through drawing links between the regular worship of the church and the peak experiences that can often occur at such events.

GATHERINGS IN SCRIPTURE

While the different kinds of events and gatherings practiced today find no exact parallel in Scripture, the Old Testament does point to the importance of festivals and sacred places among God's people. The New Testament, in contrast, downplays the significance of sacred places but retains a stress on the importance of community. Pilgrimage also features in Christian history, while the development of camps and festivals allow other ways for young people today to get away from ordinary life and encounter God.

---

2. Festivals in this chapter—aside from our discussion of the Old Testament festivals—refers not to the festivals of the Christian year, such as Christmas, Palm Sunday, or Good Friday, but rather to a large gathering of people who come together for a limited time to listen to speakers and music.

Within Judaism, the three great festivals were Passover, Pentecost, and Tabernacles.[3] Originally harvest festivals, each became associated with key events in Israel's history. Passover was linked to the exodus from Egypt, the time when God "passed over" the people of God and judged the Egyptians (Exod 12). Pentecost, at least in later Jewish history, was associated with the giving of the law at Sinai, a possible parallel that Luke may exploit in his depiction of the giving of the Spirit at Pentecost (Acts 2).[4] Tabernacles was associated with the wilderness wanderings, when the people of God would "tabernacle" in tents in the wildness.

While other festivals were also honored by the Jews,[5] the three great festivals all included a pilgrimage to Jerusalem. The biblical texts call for an annual trip to Jerusalem for each festival (Exod 23:14–17; 34:23; Deut 16:16–17), and this may have been possible for Jews living in the land of Israel. John's gospel, for instance, indicates that Jesus took several trips to Jerusalem.[6] Outside of Israel, however, pilgrimage to Jerusalem may have taken place just once in a lifetime. Whether from Israel or further afield, Jews flocked to Jerusalem for festivals, and the population of the city swelled massively at such times.

Pilgrimage in Israel, then, was to Jerusalem, with the significance of the city emphasized throughout the Old Testament. Jerusalem was the chosen site of God's presence, the place where God dwelt (Pss 76:2; 84; 135:21) While God filled the heavens, God had also condescended to fill the temple of God (1 Kgs 8:10). The temple was where God had called for sacrifices to be offered, and where God had promised to hear his people.[7]

As Jews approached the city of Jerusalem as pilgrims, many would have sung or recited the "Pilgrimage Psalms" (Pss 120–134).[8] Such psalms encouraged an attitude of expectation and awe among pilgrims drawing close to God. Jerusalem was the place to encounter God, since Jerusa-

---

3. For a brief discussion of these three festivals and their significance, see Ferguson, *Backgrounds of Early Christianity*, 521–26.

4. For a discussion of this possibility, see Witherington, *Acts of the Apostles*, 130–31.

5. See Ferguson, *Backgrounds of Early Christianity*, 525–26.

6. While the Synoptic Gospels focus on Jesus' single trip to Jerusalem, John's depiction of several trips to Jerusalem makes good historical sense (Smalley, *John*, 23–24).

7. Dunn describes the "Land focussed in Temple" as one of the "four pillars of Second Temple Judaism," alongside monotheism, election, and covenant (Dunn, *Parting of the Ways*, 42–47). See also Wright, *Jesus and the Victory of God*, 406–12.

8. On the role of such psalms, and for what they reveal about worship during the festivals, see Anderson, *Living World*, 558–66.

lem—as the psalmist proclaims—was God's "resting place for ever" (Ps 134:13–14).

While the Old Testament emphasizes the importance of pilgrimage to the holy city, the New Testament minimizes its significance. In his ministry, Jesus points to the temple as under God's judgement, and so no longer the site of God's presence with his people (Matt 24:1–2).[9] The real temple of God is found in Jesus himself; Jesus is the site of God's dwelling place (Matt 12:1–11).[10] As John's gospel particularly emphasizes, Jesus is the one in whom all the festivals of the Old Testament find their fulfillment.[11] Since the Spirit dwells in believers, Paul also treats the church as God's temple (1 Cor 3:16–17), set apart and holy, and also the site of divine encounter.[12] Hebrews also explicitly critiques the place of the temple, seeing its cult as no longer required in the light of the Christ-event (Heb 7:1—10:18).[13]

For the New Testament writers, then, Jerusalem and its temple was no longer the primary site of God's presence. Instead, God's presence was encountered in Jesus and in the gatherings of his people.[14] Following Jesus' example (Mark 1:35), the early Christians may have still sought out quiet places to pray and worship God, but they did not need to gather in a particular place to encounter God. The true worshipers of God, said Jesus, worship him in "Spirit and in truth" (John 4:24), not at temples or mountains.

While early Christians seemed to have avoided pilgrimage, we do find occasions when Christians gather together in large groups for specific occasions. Like modern camps or festivals, these would be times when Christians would journey from their usual place of worship to gather with a larger group to encounter God. The early chapters of Acts record Christians coming together in the temple while also meeting in their homes (Acts

9. While there are a variety of interpretations of Jesus actions in the temple court (Matt 21:12), one interpretation is that this was an "acted parable of Judgement," and so a parable that fit with Jesus' many warnings about the destruction of the temple (Wright, *Jesus and the Victory of God*, 413–28).

10. Ibid., 423–26.

11. On this point, see Rainbow, *Johannine Theology*, 61–62.

12. Paul also treats individual Christians as "temples of the Holy Spirit" (1 Cor 6:19–20), though the emphasis of his letters tends to be on the communal dimension of life in Christ.

13. For a richly theological account of how the Christian community saw itself as a temple of God's presence, see Beale, *New Testament Biblical Theology*, 592–648.

14. For a historical discussion of the key texts on the temple in the New Testament, and a demonstration that the early Christian view of the temple undermined its key role within Second Temple Judaism, see Dunn, *Parting of the Ways*, 49–128.

2:43–47), while Christians in other cities might meet together as a "whole church" (1 Cor 14:23) as well as in individual house churches.[15]

The early Christian experience was one of intimate community and love, but churches struggle to emulate that experience in today's very different context.[16] Events and gatherings, however, can provide an intensive experience of such a community in a way that can approach early Christianity.

The potential benefit of pilgrimage for Christians emerged in the first few centuries of the church, as followers of Jesus began to visit sites of the apostles and early martyrs, as well as sites associated with the ministry of Jesus.[17] In the fourth century CE, Jerome defended the practice of pilgrimage, providing a theological rationale for traveling to such places. Pilgrimage continued throughout the Middle Ages, but its theological rationale was questioned during the Reformation, with the Reformers particularly concerned about its potential abuse. Although later Protestants continued to be suspicious of pilgrimage, more recent years have seen Christians across the denominations praising the formative power of pilgrimage. Pilgrimage sites include places such as Jerusalem, Taizé, and Iona, while pilgrimage trails include the famous Camino de Santiago.

Other kinds of events and gatherings that feature in today's context include camps and festivals. While the first Christian camps may have taken place in the nineteenth century, they grew and developed throughout the twentieth, and became a staple for churches and youth groups, especially in the US. While having some parallels with earlier rallies, Christian festivals, where people meet together around music, worship and talks, are a more recent innovation.

The biblical support for events and gatherings might draw on the Old Testament traditions of pilgrimage, as well as the early Christian stress on community, something that events and gatherings value highly. Further support for the practical impact of such events, however, is found in Christian history. While pilgrimage has a long historical pedigree, camps and festivals also have the potential to shape the formation of youth.

15. As Banks notes, however, even the "whole church" meeting would be relatively small by today's standards (*Paul's Idea*, 36).

16. As Frazee argues in *The Connecting Church*, Christian community today is often hindered by individualism, isolation and consumerism.

17. The following discussion draws on Inge, *Christian Theology of Place*, 91–122.

EVENTS, GATHERINGS, AND YOUNG PEOPLE

In the contemporary world, "getting away" is part of life for the majority of young people. Within schools, camps provide a time to join the school community in a different setting. Clubs like the Scouts offer opportunities to experience the outdoors and develop skills, while music camps and sports camps offer concentrated times for young people to develop the skills they love. On a smaller scale, families get away for events or occasions, such as holidays, birthdays, and family reunions.

In Christian youth work, getting away to a different kind of space—camps, festivals, or pilgrimages—can offer a formational space for young people, occasions when God breaks into the lives of youth. As Dean and Foster note, such events are "dehabituating"; they take us away from our usual routine and "make us alert to Christ both by attuning us to God's signal and by tuning out a lot of spiritual static."[18]

The use of camps within youth groups is widespread. The National Study of Youth and Religion in the US shows that more than a third of all teenagers have attended a religious summer camp at least once (including well over half of all religious teens), and well over a quarter have attended multiple times.[19] Many Northern Europeans and Scandinavians participate in confirmation camps, which have become an important part of their culture.[20]

While some scholars are sceptical of the impact of camps on long-term faith formation,[21] others have argued for their lasting spiritual effect. In the US, people who attended Christian summer camps were more likely to be participants in small groups, such as Bible studies, prayer groups, and campus fellowships.[22]

Camps are also places where Christian community can be experienced, possibly for the first time. As Venable and Joy argue, it is the sense of community in the conscious presence of God that helps change lives.[23] As well as providing immersion in community life, camps provide fertile ground for the

18. Dean and Foster, *Godbearing Life*, 118.

19. Smith and Denton, *Soul Searching*, 54

20. Schweitzer et al., eds., *Youth, Religion and Confirmation*.

21. Yust challenges researches to show evidence of the long-lasting effect of camps, since the "spiritual high" they may help to create can quickly fade ("Creating an Idyllic World," 182–183).

22. Sorenson, "Summer Camp Experience," 28.

23. Venable and Joy, *How to Use Camping Experiences*.

growth of friendships and mentoring relationships.[24] If young people return to the same camp, these relationships can be refreshed and renewed, and may extend beyond the life of the camp. Those who act as leaders or counselors at such camps can also find their own faith revitalized.[25]

The rise of Christian festivals offers a different kind of experience to faith. In the United Kingdom, festivals such as New Wine and Spring Harvest draw families and youth groups from across the nation. Other festivals, such as Soul Survivor and Rock Nations, focus specifically on young people, drawing thousands each year.

Such events, in which energizing and youth-friendly worship is a typical feature, provide young people a location for encounters with God, with such encounters demonstrating the validity of their faith. The experience of God makes faith seem even more plausible, as does the experience of worshiping alongside thousands of others. Young people, in fact, testify that encounters with God happen more regularly at such events than in their normal local church programs.[26] Those who did have such encounters are also more likely to participate in the church upon their return.

Festivals also provide a space in which young people can explore their questions and doubts about God. In cultures like Britain where faith and church are perceived negatively,[27] festivals provide places where young people can explore God-talk and its relevance for their lives, as well as their doubts and questions about faith.[28]

A final example of an event or gathering is that of pilgrimage.[29] During a pilgrimage, a group of young people will travel to a sacred site, a place known for its spiritual significance within the life of the church. Sometimes

---

24. One 2006 US study of more than 7,500 campers at 80 camps (not specifically faith camps) identified "supportive relationships" as a camp's greatest asset (American Camp Association, "Inspirations," 1).

25. As Sorenson notes, the values expressed in the camps—"inclusivity, authenticity, and spiritual depth"—are also those highly valued by emerging adults ("Summer Camp Experience," 31).

26. Emery-Wright, *Now That Was Worship*, 24, 91.

27. Ibid., 65.

28. The failure of churches to allow young people to share such doubts may explain why some people feel so alienated from church. See Kinnaman, *You Lost Me*, 134; Sorenson, "Summer Camp Experience," 32–33.

29. For a discussion of pilgrimage as a "practice of transcendence," see Dean, *Practicing Passion*, 196–221.

spiritual formation will happen on the pilgrimage itself,[30] while in other settings the focus will be engaging with the community living or active at the site. While camps will often move into a particular space for a period, sites of pilgrimage tend to be active throughout the year, and will often have a small community present within them.

The potential of pilgrimages to provoke spiritual change can be considered through the lens of "transformative education," an approach to learning that emphasizes the way in which "disorientation" can lead to a shift in assumptions and perception about life.[31] If those experiencing such disorientation are given space for critical reflection , sometimes helped by a facilitator, this can help them make sense of the experience.[32]

One study of emerging adults (ages eighteen to twenty-four) who traveled to Taizé revealed the transformative learning that took place.[33] Taizé, an ecumenical monastic community of brothers in France, models a way of worship and a rhythm of life that was particularly disorienting to those who attended the pilgrimage, and this was reflected in their journal entries. While many of the students at the beginning of the week were uncomfortable and even angry, their attitudes began to change by the middle of the week, including around the use of silence, faith practices, and images of God. Six months after the trip, participants spoke of how God had powerfully used the trip in their lives. The experience was particularly transformative for those participants who incorporated the experience at Taizé into daily practice on their own and with friends. Those who failed to put the change into practice still revealed different attitudes and hopes for further growth, but were somewhat frustrated that the change was not as lasting as they desired.

Events and gatherings, then, are opportunities to encounter God in fresh ways. Camps provide a time to build community in the midst of friends and mentors; festivals assure young people that they are not alone as they worship with hundreds of others; and pilgrimages are an opportunity

30. In her study of teenagers and faith, Lytch notes that "religious experiences seem to happen most often on retreats" (*Choosing Church*, 60).

31. The key thinker in this area is Jack Mezirow. For an overview of his approach, see his "Learning to Think Like an Adult: Core Concepts of Transformation Theory," in Mezirow and Associates, *Learning as Transformation*, 3–34. For a discussion of how "transformative education" can apply to adult theological education, and how it links to Lonergan's theological method, see Fleischer, "Mezirow's Theory of Transformative Learning."

32. Merriam, "Studying Transformative Learning," in Taylor et al., *Handbook of Transformative Learning*, 65.

33. Emery-Wright, "Study of Liminality."

to encounter more deeply the transforming grace of God. By moving away from the familiar and into the unfamiliar, young people are opened up to fresh possibilities of transformation.[34]

DEEPENING FAITH THROUGH EVENTS AND GATHERINGS

Given the importance of events and gatherings, how can church leaders, youth ministers, and parents help young people engage with them?

Our first suggestion is that church leaders and youth ministers prioritize such events and gatherings for young people, even for those who might be reluctant to risk leaving home! As we have seen, such events can be deeply significant for adolescents. They can also help young people become aware of the catholicity of their faith—the way in which Christianity has different expressions and draws different people into its fold, all of whom can encounter the living Christ at is center.

In prioritizing such events, it is important to think carefully about what will be the best fit, both for the young person and for the church. As we have seen, camps, events, and festivals provide different kinds of experiences for young people, and different stages or ages may be a better fit for some rather than others. The theological assumptions and the faith practices that the event or gathering offers are also worth considering. Camps, for instance, will differ widely in the mix of activities and faith practices they value, and most church leaders will value at least some congruency between the church and the event.[35]

There is great value too in a church creating a long-standing relationship with an event or a gathering. As young people move up through youth groups, knowing that their first year of high school is when the "Cardiff Camp" happens, for example, will build positive associations between the camp and growth into adolescence.

Our second suggestion is that churches should work hard to help young people integrate their experience of God at an event or gathering with the life of their church at home. This is particularly important because

34. Victor and Edith Turner describe the transition from familiar places and patterns to sacred spaces in terms of "liminality," and show that such "liminal places" are particular potent spheres for achieving a deep sense of community, within which change can take place (Turner and Turnter, *Image and Pilgrimage*). For a reading of camps in terms of "liminal spaces," see McCabe "Who Needs a Holiday?"

35. For an interesting study in the way that a theological framework affected the experience of young people at a rally, see Haskell and Flatt, "When Youth Experience God."

there is a risk that events or gatherings could become substitutes for life in the church, with young people depending solely on them for their spiritual nurture.[36] Such young people can go from event to event, continually seeking the next spiritual high but without grounding it in the everyday ways in which God grows his people.

While the church cannot duplicate the experience of God the young person may have had at the event or gathering, it should seek to support young people following the event. This can happen when a church gives young people an opportunity to voice their experience or fresh commitment to the church at large, and for the church to celebrate it. The local church can also provide young people with opportunities for leadership and service that will help their faith to grow further.

The experience that the young person has received away from the church can also impact the church in hugely positive ways. In fact, encounters with God at special events are vital to maintaining local faith communities.[37] The excitement and vision of the young people breathes new life back into the church, demonstrating the integrity of what is being proclaimed in their own experience. These experiences, in other words, provide something of an answer to the problem of the faithful hardworking church at Ephesus. Seeing the way in which young people can passionately fall in love with God—even at camp!—can encourage others in the church to fan the flame of their "first love" (Rev 2:1–3).

CONCLUSION

Events and gatherings provide fertile ground for spiritual change, but, like all such networks, they cannot guarantee that such change will happen. Church leaders and parents can pray that such experiences will impact the lives of their youth, and, when they do, should nurture the growth that has taken place.

Like all of the networks, events and gatherings also need to be situated within the broader ecology of faith. While they are primarily places where young people receive input into their faith, it is helpful to also consider ways to encourage young people to live out their faith proactively, as our next chapter demonstrates.

36. As Dean and Foster note, such mountaintop experiences cannot by themselves support lasting faith, although they can act as entry points into other sorts of relationships and practices that do shape faith (*Godbearing Life*, 85).

37. Rappaport, *Ritual and Religion*, 396.

PUTTING IT INTO PRACTICE

- Encourage young people to share their testimony of how they experienced an event or gathering. What was it that was transformative? What changed them?

- Consider attending an event as a church group, perhaps encouraging all to attend a church weekend away. If encountering God away from home happens in the presence of church members of all ages, this has the added benefit of creating a strong link with the church community at home.

- Consider encouraging young people attend events that might stretch their faith in new ways. For example if they have attended a large youth worship event a number of times, they might be encouraged to consider Taizé or a retreat.

FURTHER READING

Jones, Andrew. *Pilgrimage: The Journey to Remembering Our Story*. Abingdon: BRF, 2011.

Jones explores the potential of pilgrimage to renew and refresh faith, including through "remembering God's story," and argues that the church has a lot to learn from this historic practice.

Newby, Vicki, ed. *Camps, Retreats, Missions, & Service Ideas for Youth Groups*. Grand Rapids: Zondervan, 1997.

A helpful book that gives youth leaders almost two hundred ideas for helping to plan camps and retreats (and missions or service trips) with young people.

Venable, Stephen F., and Donald M. Joy. *How to Use Camping Experiences in Religious Education*. Birmingham: Religious Education, 1998.

Venebale and Joy offer a useful guide to making use of the camp experience, particularly noting its potential to create and sustain Christian community in the presence of God.

9

Mission and Service
Transforming Faith

Mission . . . is faith in action. It is the acting out by proclamation and by endur-
ance, through all the events of history, of the faith that the kingdom of God has
drawn near.

Lesslie Newbigin[1]

INTRODUCTION

MANY YEARS AGO, I (Steve) led a short-term mission project with a group
of young people within the church. We traveled together to an economically deprived area of Appalachia, where together we sought to serve the
community. As well as getting to know the residents, we helped to build
new houses (replacing the shacks that many lived in), put on classes for
young people, and painted old buildings.

On the first day of the mission, Amy, sixteen at the time, said she felt
like she was "gift-wrapping trash." Looking around the state of the community, it seemed that she and the team could make scarcely any difference
at all. During the week, Amy worked hard, putting up walls, painting buildings, and forming relationships with the locals. By the time the mission had
come to an end, Amy spoke of the privilege she felt in being involved. She
had learned to see the treasure in the midst of the mess, and had begun to

1. Newbigin, *Open Secret*, 43.

love the people she had not even known a week earlier. Through her service of others, Amy had changed.

Going on mission, or serving in mission, can be profoundly transformative for young people. It can help young people live out the faith they confess and expose young people to those who are different. While mission has its risks, it can open up young people to God's transforming grace.

While the exact nature of mission and missions continues to be debated,[2] Christopher Wright's definition is particularly helpful: "Mission, from the point of view of our human endeavour, means the committed participation of God's people in the purposes of God for the redemption of the whole creation."[3] Such participation involves both evangelism and work for social justice, proclaiming the gospel and living lives of love and compassion.[4] The both/and approach is reflected in documents from the World Council of Churches as well as from the evangelical Lausanne Movement.[5] It also offers a helpful corrective to those youth ministers who focus exclusively on either evangelism or social justice.[6]

While such mission is part of the daily call for Christians, our focus in this chapter will be on how church leaders, youth ministers, and parents intentionally seek to create corporate opportunities for young people to reach out in mission. This might include local projects as well as short-term missions, whether domestic or international. Such mission will typically include a service element, and will often provide opportunities for young people to share their faith with those they meet.

This chapter begins by exploring mission in Scripture, drawing on recent efforts at a missional reading of Scripture. We next give an overview of evidence for the effectiveness of mission and service in deepening faith.

2. A seminal text on the theme remains Bosch, *Transforming Mission*, which describes five different "models of mission."

3. Wright, *Mission of God*, 67.

4. While some missiologists adopt a more limited view of mission as "proclaiming the gospel," such as Ferdinando ("Mission") and DeYoung and Gilbert (*What Is the Mission of the Church?*), a biblical hermeneutic of mission can also support the both/and approach, as demonstrated by C. Wright, *Mission of God*, and N. T. Wright, *Surprised by Hope*.

5. World Council of Churches, "Together Towards Life"; Lausanne Movement, "Lausanne Covenant." See also the "five marks of mission" within the Anglican Communion, which similarly embrace a holistic approach (Anglican Communion, "Marks of Mission").

6. For a defense of the both/and approach in youth work, see especially Clark and Powell, *Deep Justice in a Broken World*.

We end by describing two ways in which churches can make the most of mission trips and service projects for young people.

MISSION IN SCRIPTURE

While some missiological approaches come to the Bible in search of the proof texts for mission, more recent approaches focus on the biblical depiction of the mission of God (*Missio Dei*)[7] and God's calling of a people to participate in his purposes for the world.[8] Such an approach traces mission as a theme throughout the whole Bible and points to the importance of holistic mission that reflects God's reconciling work in creation as well as redemption.

The mission of God can be found at the very start of the Bible in God's creation of Adam and Eve. Made in the image of God, Adam and Eve are given dominion over all creation, and invited into relationship with God and one another (Gen 1:26–31; 2:18–25). According to G. K. Beale, the garden of Eden also functions as a microcosm of the temple, the place of God's glorious presence.[9] Adam and Eve are appointed as "priest-kings" of Eden, and called to inhabit the earth, thereby filling all of creation with God's glory.[10] The fall of Adam and Eve represents a rupture in God's intent to fill the earth with his glory, and sets in motion God's intent to redeem his fallen creation.

God's design for redemption begins in Israel's story with the call of Abraham in Genesis 12:1–3.[11] God calls Abraham to leave his home and set off to a new land, promising to make of him a great nation. God also gives him a covenantal promise: "I will bless those who bless you, and the one who curses you I will curse; and in you all the families of the earth shall be blessed" (12:3). Such a text points to the way in which God works through a particular people to work for the blessing of many, a promise ultimately fulfilled in the person of Christ (Gal 3:15–18).

7. The *missio Dei* ("mission of God") is a hugely significant theme in contemporary missiology. For a history of the term, see Laing, "*Missio Dei*."

8. Bosch, *Transforming Mission*; Wright, *Mission of God*; Cardoza-Orlandi, *Mission*; Goheen, *Light to the Nations*.

9. See Beale, *New Testament Biblical Theology*, 29–87; and *Temple and the Church's Mission*.

10. Beale, *Temple and the Church's Mission*, 82.

11. For a thorough discussion, see Wright, *Mission of God*, 191–221.

As the story of Israel unfolds, God's people are set apart as a "nation of priests" (Exod 19:4–6), and called to reflect the holiness of God in the midst of the nations (Leviticus).[12] Israel fails time after time to reflect God's holiness, and the cycle of judgement and redemption inevitably follows. While Israel is called to witness to God by its holiness, there is no "missional mandate" in the Old Testament, no calling for the people of Israel to evangelize the nations.[13] There is, however, a promise in the prophets that God will one day draw all nations to himself (Isa 19:13; 59:18—60:6; Zech 8:21; Jer 3:17), and so fulfill the promise to Abraham.

The central redemptive event in the Old Testament, the exodus, points to the holistic nature of the *Missio Dei*.[14] God's mission to redeem Israel from slavery was not simply spiritual, but also economic and social. It embraced the salvation of bodies, and not just saving souls. If this is the case, then the exodus event gives something of a paradigm for mission; "exodus-shaped redemption demands exodus-shaped mission."[15] Just as God's redemption of the Israelites from Egypt involved every sphere of existence, so mission today should be similarly broad.

In the New Testament, God's plan to redeem his creation is focused on the mission of the Son. John's gospel announces that "the Word became flesh and lived among us, and we have seen his glory" (1:14a). Each of the gospels point to Jesus as "God with us,"[16] and the rest of the New Testament similarly emphasizes the coming of the Son in human history. Paul explains that "when the fullness of time had come, God sent his Son" (Gal 4:4a); Hebrews begins with a declaration that God has "spoken to us by a Son" (1:2); and 2 Peter assures readers that the "coming of Lord Jesus" was truly witnessed by those who were there (2 Pet 1:16–18).

Alongside the coming of the Son, the New Testament describes the coming of the Spirit in fulfillment of the prophetic promises (Joel 2). While the Spirit was present in the Old Testament, the Pentecost account points to the eschatological pouring out of the Spirit on all people (Acts 2:14–36), including Gentiles (Acts 10:34–48). The Spirit is also given to guide believers

12. Goheen, *Light to the Nations*, 49–60.

13. This is a point broadly attested, and explains why missiologists have often ignored the Old Testament in favour of the New with its clear instructions to go out in mission.

14. For this argument, and the points that follow, see Wright, *Mission of God*, 265–68. Wright similarly argues that the Jubilee is a model of "restoration" that should guide our thinking on mission today (289–323).

15. Ibid., 275.

16. For a recent demonstration of this point, see Hays, *Reading Backwards*.

into all truth (John 16:4b–15), and is a foretaste of the coming kingdom. As Beale also argues, the coming of the Spirit at Pentecost shapes God's people to be an end-time temple, a place of God's presence within the world.[17]

The mission of God's people in the New Testament takes place against the backdrop of this *Missio Dei*, God's own redemptive work. Unlike the Old Testament, mission in the New involves going and proclaiming the good news. Mission becomes centrifugal and not just centripetal.

Jesus' own (earthly) mission was one of missiological engagement.[18] Jesus proclaimed in word and deed the good news of the kingdom, God's reign over his people. The kingdom of God involved reconciliation to God and to others, and also meant following Jesus. While Jesus' mission was focused on the "lost sheep of Israel" (Matt 10:5–6), Jesus also pointed in his parables to a future Gentile mission (Matt 8:11–12; Luke 13:28–29).

Jesus also sent his followers out on mission to bring peace, healing, and the good news of the kingdom. His selection of twelve disciples was a symbolic reconstitution of God's people, but the twelve were also chosen to "fish for people" (Mark 1:17). In Matthew 10, Jesus sends out the twelve to tell the good news of the kingdom throughout Israel, and to demonstrate its presence by the miraculous deeds (10:5–15). Even at this period, Jesus expected his followers to encounter resistance and hostility, and so Jesus also warns his disciples of "coming persecutions" (10:1–25).

Jesus' mission ended in suffering, and found its climax in the cross. Soteriologically, as well as historically, the cross was the "endpoint" of Jesus' mission (Mark 10:45). Through his death, Jesus defeated sin and evil and opened the way to reconciliation with God. Jesus' resurrection is the divine declaration that the new age has come and a further unveiling of Jesus' identity.

After his resurrection, Jesus calls his disciples to take the message of the gospel to all nations, most famously in the great commission (Matt 28:18–20). Followers of Jesus were to make disciples in every nation, calling them to baptism and teaching them the way of Christ. As Acts shows, the Spirit empowered the early Christians to reach out in mission to the very ends of the earth. The church's way of life was one that reflected the kingdom—a kingdom of righteousness, peace, and joy (Rom 14:17)—while its message pointed to the salvation available in Christ.

---

17. Beale, *New Testament Biblical Theology*, 592–613.

18. For a detailed analysis of mission in the life of Jesus, see Schnabel, *Early Christian Mission*, 1:175–386.

Paul, the apostle to the Gentiles, also reached out in mission through proclaiming the gospel, the story of God's redemptive work through Christ's death and resurrection (Rom 1:3–4; 1 Cor 15:3–8).[19] Paul had been converted from a persecutor of the church to a faithful advocate, and planted churches across the Mediterranean. While Paul's focus was primarily on the Christ-event, he also called Christians to follow the way of Christ, loving neighbors, treating others with compassion, and acting with kindness to all (Rom 12:9–21; Gal 5:13–15).

Mission also required the transformation of the church. As gentiles came to faith, tension and conflict arose between Jewish and gentile followers of Jesus. Paul had to fight against Jewish believers telling gentiles that they had to be circumcised (Gal 6:11–16) and against gentiles treating Jews with arrogance or a sense of superiority (Rom 11:11–24). Paul invited both Jews and gentiles to be transformed by the Spirit in their midst, and to accept one another as servants of the same Lord (Rom 14:1–12). Those who saw themselves as strong in faith particularly needed to look out for the weak, following the way of Christ who gave himself up for others (Rom 14:13—15:6).

While the exodus points to a holistic expression of mission, the New Testament associates mission primarily with the proclamation of the gospel.[20] Living the way of the gospel, however, meant living the way of Jesus, a path of love and compassion towards others. While the church's mission was focused on proclaiming the gospel, the community called into being by the gospel shared God's love and grace with the world. Canonically, then, a strong case can be made for seeing mission as involving both evangelism and good works, loving others and seeking to "bless" all in the world.[21]

Within the Christian tradition, engaging in mission is also associated with spiritual transformation. As Richard Foster argues, the "social justice tradition" is one of the great streams of Christian faith, and includes figures such as Vincent de Paul, William Booth, Dorothy Day, and Mother

19. For a thorough description of Paul's missiological approach, see Schnabel, *Early Christian Mission*, 2:921–1485.

20. See ibid., 1379–1419, 1562–68. See also DeYoung and Gilbert, *What Is the Mission of the Church?*

21. To preserve the focus in the New Testament, some writers distinguish between the mission of the church, focused on proclaiming the gospel, and the mission of Christians, which includes social justice and works of mercy (as well as evangelism). See, for example, Keller's distinction between the institutional church and the organic church in *Generous Justice*, 144.

Teresa.[22] Through social justice, "God develops in us the compassion to love our neighbor freely and develops in our world a place where justice and righteousness prevail."[23] The "evangelical" tradition is equally valuable, and focuses on the urgency of gospel proclamation.[24] Reaching out in evangelism can also transform the evangelists, stirring their passion to see others love God and live for him and also humbling them as they notice God's work in the lives of others.

The way in which mission and evangelism can be spiritually transformative is also reflected in John Wesley's description of the means of grace.[25] For Wesley, such means included "works of mercy," such as compassion and seeking justice for others. Through such practices, God's grace transforms Christians! In Wesleyan theology, evangelism can similarly be regarded as a means of grace, driven as it is by compassion for another. Evangelism and service, then, are not simply acts we do in response to God's grace, but are also practices through which we receive God's grace.[26]

MISSION AND FAITH

Given the biblical importance of mission, it is unsurprising that many youth workers recognize its importance in the spiritual formation of youth. Indeed, many youth workers, at least in the American context, see part of their job as taking youth on missions.[27] While the number of young people involved in service or mission is still far from a majority,[28] it is nonetheless an important priority of many working with youth today.

22. Foster, *Streams of Living Water*, 135–83.

23. Ibid., 182.

24. Ibid., 185–233. For Foster, "evangelical" is a broader category than those associated with evangelicalism today, and so he cites figures such as Augustine of Hippo, Thomas Aquinas, and C. S. Lewis as notable figures in this tradition.

25. See Wesley's sermon on the "means of grace": Wesley, "Sermon 16." See also the discussion of Sanders, *Wesley on the Christian Life*, 173–90; and United Methodist Church, "Wesleyan Means of Grace."

26. Walton also argues that mission is a "primary location for formation" (*Disciples Together*, 1–15).

27. Trinitapoli and Vaisey, "Transformative Role," 123; Priest and Priest, "They See Everything," 61

28. The NSRY study found that only 30 percent of adolescents are involved in a mission or service project (Smith and Denton, *Soul Searching*, 69).

There are various forms that the mission might take.[29] On a local level, mission might involve a variety of service projects. Churches, youth groups, and parents can work with teens to help a local homeless shelter, or to organize a clean-up of a local park. In the UK, the Hope Together initiative encourages churches across the countries—including their youth groups—to see the missional potential of such service projects.[30] Serving the local community is a way of embodying the gospel, as well as creating opportunities for evangelism.

Research into such service projects shows that they are correlated to a wide range of positive impacts. Youth are more likely to develop empathy and compassion in such contexts, particularly if role models work alongside them.[31] Being involved in service also helps young people grow spirituality.[32] Those involved in such ministries become more likely to engage in personal faith practices, including prayer and Bible reading, as well as participating more regularly in church.[33]

At a local level, mission can also involve encouraging young people to share their faith with others. While some may question whether young people are mature enough to do so, sharing faith or evangelism is the calling of every disciple, young or old (1 Pet 3:15). In many instances, young people are in fact better placed to reach out in evangelism, and including a focus on evangelistic events and opportunities alongside other mission outreach is a good way to recognize the priority of evangelism within the church's mission.[34] Examples might include helping to set up a youth rally, inviting friends to events at church, or performing street drama that invites conversations on faith.

Evangelism helps people grow because young people have the chance to become more articulate about their faith, and so more confident in owning it.[35] As Greg Stier argues, encouraging young people to share their

29. For a discussion of mission in a British youth work context, see Terry Linhart, "Mission," in Nash and Whitehead, eds., *Christian Youth Work*, 176–86.

30. See Hope Together, "Hope in Our Villages and Towns."

31. See the findings of Wuthnow on this issue, summarized in Sheer et al., "Role of Community Service."

32. Ibid.

33. Ibid., 50.

34. See Bosch's description of evangelism as the "heart of mission" in Bosch, "Evangelism." While Wright recognizes that mission is far more than evangelism (as does Bosch), he too sees it as central (Wright, *Mission of God*, 276–78).

35. The sociologist Ines Jindra writes of the importance of this re-storying of life in

faith, to point others to Jesus, gives them excitement about their faith.[36] It encourages them to step out of their comfort zone and, in so doing, find that God meets them there too.[37]

As well as local ways of engaging in mission, many churches involve their youth in short-term mission trips (also called "faith-based service projects"). Such trips involve traveling to another location (either domestic or international) and spending up to a month in service of a community that is not one's own.[38] The mission team is usually relatively small (six to twenty-five), and typically includes a majority of young people, although at times it may be intergenerational. The mission itself can include activities such as running a vacation Bible school or day camp for children, a building project in an area of need, an urban project not far from home, or any other number of activities seeking to help others.

Adolescents who go on such trips can find them, as one study puts it, a "formative—even transcendent—experience."[39] The study showed that short-term mission increased the religious participation of adolescents as well as helping them solidify their religious beliefs.[40] Such trips also meant that young people felt closer to God, and were more positive about evangelism.[41]

Spiritual transformation can also take place as young people encounter those who are different from them, a common experience in short-term missions![42] Such encounters provide an opportunity to develop "cultural intelligence," the ability to empathize with and so more deeply love those who are different than us.[43] This requires more than simply learning about

---

order to foster a change in worldview (*New Model of Religious Conversion*, 67).

36. Stier, "Gospel Advancing View of Youth Ministry," in Clark, *Youth Ministry*, 3–16; and Stier, *Gospelize Your Youth Ministry*.

37. On the manner of such evangelism and witness, see the helpful discussion of the "practice of witness" in Dean and Foster, *Godbearing Life*, 173–84.

38. Most trips, in fact, are under two weeks (Priest and Priest, "They See Everything," 56).

39. Trinitapoli and Vaisey, "Transformative Role of Religious Experience," 140.

40. Ibid., 121.

41. Ibid., 138–39. See also Powell and Clark, *Sticky Faith*, 129–30.

42. Encountering the other is not, however, limited to such mission trips. In a pluralistic world, young people will often encounter the other in the everyday, such as at school or clubs. Such encounters can also have an impact on others.

43. Livermore, *Cultural Intelligence*.

other cultures; it also requires inward transformation,[44] a transformation that sees others as loved by God.[45] Prejudices, stereotypes, and unquestioned assumptions of other people are challenged when we meet real people of other cultures and faiths.[46]

Engaging young people in mission also recognizes that they too are disciples in their own right. Rather than simply being objects of mission or "spiritual development programs," young people are those called by Christ to reach out in compassion to the poor and needy, to share the good news of the coming of Christ, and to join in God's mission of redemption in the world.

TRANSFORMING FAITH THROUGH MISSION

Engaging with others in mission, then, is a further network for faith formation, a way in which young people can be transformed by the grace of God. Mission teaches young people that reaching out in love to others is part of God's call to disciples. Involvement in mission is not just for adults, but for all who choose to follow in the footsteps of Jesus of Nazareth.

Churches can capitalize on the potential of this network by, first, creating opportunities for mission to take place. This might involve a local service project, since a range of needs are present in every community. Taking a community audit can help a church identify where they might begin. While some opportunities for service might be a one-off, such as helping at a Christmas shelter, others might involve an ongoing commitment, like regularly volunteering at a food bank.

Churches and youth leaders can also promote short-term mission as a way of serving others. As well as providing an opportunity for such service, they also allow young people to get away with a community of other Christians. Church and youth leaders can research the best fit for the church and think about how best to partner with existing Christian communities in the area of service. If the same church sends groups to the same area each year, then this will allow young people to get a better sense of the particular context and also come to know the community well.

44. Ibid., 12

45. Ibid., 242.

46. It is, of course, not always the case that such trips lead to genuine encounter with others, and so, as we call for below, churches need to ensure best practice when organizing them. See Livermore, *Eyes Wide Open*.

Churches can also use mission opportunities to build other kinds of networks. If parents are involved with their children in such projects, this provides another way in which faith is modeled within the home.[47] Encouraging other adults besides the youth worker to attend mission trips also provides a setting in which mentoring can naturally develop.

Churches should, secondly, seek to pursue best practices in the area of mission and service. At the basic level, this involves ensuring that issues of safeguarding are taken into account. Being clear about the setting of a mission, and what will be expected of the young people, is also important.

If involving youth in evangelistic techniques, care needs to be taken to help young people share their faith with wisdom and grace. Young people should be carefully mentored to love and respect those they speak to, and to know that it is God who does the work.

Churches especially need to be aware of the potential pitfalls of short-term missions. Some missiologists criticise such experiences since they encourage young people to have stereotypical view of those they serve.[48] Others note that young people can often treat such experiences as tourists rather than pilgrims,[49] and leave the experience without the sense of partnership that the best mission trips encourage. Given the amount of money spent on sending young people on such missions, some argue that it would better to simply give the money to those in need rather than use it for such mission trips.[50]

Despite such risks, mission trips can be spiritually transformative for those who participate and helpful for the receiving partners of the trip.[51] When churches are aware of such risks, they can ensure that young people are properly prepared before going on mission and debriefed upon their return. Preparation will involve helping young people understand the context, and also approaching the trip as an opportunity to partner with an existing Christian community rather than simply going as givers. Thinking theologically about the process of mission should also be part of the preparation and debrief.

47. On family involvement in modeling service and mission more generally, see Powell and Clark, *Sticky Faith*, 123–48.

48. Howell, "Mission to Nowhere," and Howell et al., "Should Churches Abandon."

49. Root, *Unlocking Mission and Eschatology*, 45–52.

50. Wuthnow and Offutt estimate that North American STM volunteers spent $2.7 billion on time and transportation ("Transnational Religious Connections," 218).

51. For a defense of the value of short-term missions from a missiological perspective, see Priest and Priest, "They See Everything."

CONCLUSION

Creating opportunities for service and mission can be spiritually transformative. Whether carried out in local contexts, or involving a trip to another region or country, mission can help young people live out the gospel of love and service. By serving others, young people can be transformed.

Mission and service should be connected with other practices, including worship within the church.[52] When part of a number of networks for faith formation, mission and service allow young people to grow as they engage with others, expressing love of God and love of neighbor as they do.

PUTTING IT INTO PRACTICE

- If your church's young people are not already serving the community, look for small ways to do so together with them. Looking for a one-off project might be a good place to start, such as a day of clearing up the local park.

- Explore experiences of evangelism within the youth group, and look for culturally appropriate ways to share faith within the community. This might include street art or drama, invitations to a youth event, or encouraging young people to have conversations about faith with their friends.

- If considering a short-term mission trip, be sure to focus on building relationships with those who are served. Before the trip, take time to explain the importance of partnering with others and the way in which those who are sent to others are also called to learn from them and from God.

---

52. See Walton's discussion of "the rhythm of discipleship," which involves both encountering God in the gathered church and being sent—with God—into the world (*Reflective Disciple*, 82–110).

FURTHER READING

Clark, Chap, and Kara E. Powell. *Deep Justice in a Broken World: Helping Your Kids Serve Others and Right the Wrongs around Them*. Grand Rapids: Zondervan, 2007.

> A helpful guide to a holistic view of mission and to helping young people think through issues of justice from a Christian perspective.

Livermore, David A. *Serving With Eyes Wide Open*. Grand Rapids: Baker, 2006.

> An excellent guide to planning a short-term mission that emphasizes the need for cultural intelligence when planning a mission trip.

Stier, Greg. *Gospelize Your Youth Ministry*. Arvada, CO: D2S, 2015.

> Drawing on the Acts of the Apostles, Stier provocatively argues that encouraging young people to evangelize is a key way to promote their spiritual growth.

10

The Way Forward
Adopting Networks for Faith Formation

Individual faith is unimaginable without a community of witness and support.

THOMAS ODEN[1]

INTRODUCTION

NETWORKS FOR FAITH FORMATION function as an ecology of relationships that nurture and nourish our Christian lives, and are a significant way in which God shapes us. As we noted in chapter 1, God has called us all into relationship, and formed us for relationships with others. We are shaped significantly by those we encounter and engage.

The stress on relationships is not meant to displace the personal faith of young people. Bedroom practices are deeply important, as we saw in chapter 2. Bedroom practices, however, have a symbiotic relationship with other sets of relationships. Young people embedded within communities where they see and hear prayer modeled and practiced are far more likely to pray alone in their bedrooms. And young people who read Scripture regularly are more likely to engage in Bible studies that take place within the church.

Christians can resist the social dimensions of Christian faith in a number of different ways. In the eighteenth century, John Wesley critiqued

1. Oden, *Classic Christianity*, 705.

the tendency of mystics to focus so much on the self that they neglected relationships with others. In response, Wesley wrote that there was "no holiness but social holiness."[2] God uses our interactions with others as avenues for grace and support, and to neglect such relationships is to neglect our growth in holiness.

In today's context, individualism is a further challenge to prioritizing networks for faith formation. Such individualism sees holiness as primarily an individual pursuit and resists the role of others in shaping one's faith. The stress on a personal relationship with Jesus might support such a tendency, while the growth of those embracing "spirituality without religion" is a broader cultural movement that stresses the subjectivity of the self over the authority of a text or a community.[3] The Bible, however, continues to challenge the individualism that is a pernicious temptation of Western Christians. For Christians in Scripture and today, faith is always a communal enterprise.

Finally, some Christians might resist engaging with networks for faith formation due to the hurt they have received from the church[4] or, frankly, due to the difficulty of relating to other Christians. Church leaders need to do all that they can to pastorally support those who are wavering in faith, providing space for them to continue to feel at home in the Christian community. At the same time, Christians who would rather not bother with the difficulty of Christian relationships need to be reminded that dealing with those who are difficult or challenging is one way in which God shapes us. Those seeking a Christian community that consists of people so similar to us, or so holy, that they will not cause us offense are under a dangerous delusion. As Bonhoeffer put it,

> Innumerable times a whole Christian community has broken down because it had sprung up from a wish dream. The serious Christian, set down for the first time in a Christian community, is likely to bring with him a very definite idea of what Christian life together should be and to try to realize it. But God's grace speedily shatters such dreams. Just as surely as God desires to lead us to a

2. See Runyon, *New Creation*, 113–14.

3. Such a movement is not wholly individualistic, but it certainly stresses the subjective self in a way distinct from Christianity. For one assessment of the "spiritual but not religious" movement, or post-religious spirituality more generally, see Mackenzie, "Following Jesus in a Spiritual Age."

4. This is often because the church fails to meet expectations, which is one reason for church-leaving found in Richter and Francis, *Gone but Not Forgotten*, 102–20.

knowledge of genuine Christian fellowship, so surely must we be overwhelmed by a great disillusionment with others, with Christians in general, and, if we are fortunate, with ourselves.[5]

Networks and relationships, then, are necessary for us all. Without such networks young people are unlikely to grow, while weaving a thick web of such relationships can help young people not just to survive in their faith but to flourish.

In this final chapter, we explore ways in which churches can adopt the eight networks we have discussed, particularly in their work with young people. In the first section of the chapter, we provide practical thoughts on how to evaluate a church in the light of these networks. As well as performing a simple activity around the eight networks, we suggest that incorporating theological reflection in the process can help people within the church, young and old, see what is missing and what to do about it. Finally, we explore how accepting the importance of networks for faith formation might shape different groups within the church: church leaders, youth workers, parents, congregation members, and young people themselves.

EVALUATING YOUR CHURCH

The strengths and weaknesses of a church's approach to spiritual growth—and particularly the growth of its young people—can be analyzed through the eight networks of faith formation. Table 1 below can be printed off and used as a simple tool to help with this.

5. Bonhoeffer, *Life Together*, 26–27.

Network for Formation	How are we doing?	How can we do better?
Bedroom Practices		
Church		
Family		
Friends		
Mentors		
Small Groups		
Events and Gatherings		
Mission and Service		

Table 1: Evaluating Your Networks for Faith Formation

To begin, the church leader or youth worker should fill in the table based on their own knowledge of young people within the congregation. As a next step, young people can be invited to identify which of the eight networks they can identify in their own lives. Young people will be aware of networks that the church leader or youth worker may not. They may have Christian relatives and informal mentors outside the Christian community, as well as Christian friends at school. Inviting them to think about these networks will also be a means to reflect on how they are shaped by others, which can be a source of gratitude as well as fresh insight into how their faith is formed.

One way of engaging young people with the eight networks would be to print out images of the different kind of networks that exist, such an image of a festival to represent "events and gatherings," a depiction of a soup kitchen to represent "mission and service," and an image of a prayer stool to represent "bedroom practices" (the nature of each network will need some explanation). Young people can then be asked to write on flip chart paper or Post-it notes ways in which they relate to each network. This will give a strong visual representation of the networks with which young people are connected, and which relationships are missing.

When leaders and young people have identified areas where further support might be needed, the wider congregation can get involved. Steps can be identified to fill the gaps, and explore how weaker networks can be strengthened.[6] This might involve preaching a series of sermons that touch on the different range of networks that help build faith, developing a series of small group Bible studies, or implementing changes to the running of the church.

It is also important to note that some networks are more important than others. Engaging in the worship and life of the church is a necessary network, something that is part of the ordinary way in which God shapes us, and this network should complement the importance of bedroom faith. Since parents have such a huge impact on young people, their role is also particularly important, and Christian parents should be encouraged to recognize the significance of the family as a network for faith formation.[7] Spending time with Christian friends is also a key network, one that young Christians need as they develop their ability to articulate and own their faith.

Other networks are also important but, in terms of priority, may be less so than church, family, and friends. While a larger church might be able to find opportunities or spaces for each of the eight networks, a smaller church could consider creating links with other churches or parachurch organizations. A church with just one or two teenagers, for example, might find a Christian parachurch organization that runs a small Christian group in the neighboring village and encourage their young people to go along.

One church that sought to see their community through the lens of the eight networks, St. Paul's, found it a helpful tool for identifying strengths as well as weaknesses. An Anglican church in a small market town in England, St. Paul's ran a strong youth program, but noticed that many of the young people drifted away from church and faith as they entered the late teens. With guidance from Steve, the leadership decided to analyze their church through the grid of networks for faith formation.

The exercise revealed a number of strengths. The church was strong on worship, events, and mission. It was also great at encouraging bedroom

6. At this point, it might be helpful to refer back to our suggestions of how faith formation might be strengthened in each of the eight networks.

7. Young people who come from non-Christian homes obviously need more support in nurturing faith; for them particularly, the church needs to be a family that helps them grow in faith, and the role of mentors become even more important.

faith, with young people engaging in daily prayer and Bible reading. The exercise also revealed two areas for improvement.

Firstly, it demonstrated that there was little interaction between adults in the congregation and young people. While there were occasional youth services, such events were rarely times when young and old built relationships with each other. The segregation of young and old within the church meant that the teens had few opportunities to know mentors, or to see faith lived out in the lives of others. The church began intentionally to encourage adults within the congregation to build relationships with young people, explaining the important role they had as informal mentors, while also creating further opportunities for young and old to mix.

A second weakness was that parents were not particularly involved in the development of their children's faith, and the church provided little support to help parents in this area. By recognizing this area of weakness, the church began to provide resources for parents. Some of the parents also realized for the first time the important role they could play in the faith development of their children.

THE ROLE OF THEOLOGICAL REFLECTION

While Table 1 above offers an easy-to-use tool for churches, encouraging a process of intentional theological reflection can also help churches reflect more deeply on the role of networks and relationships.[8]

This might be particularly helpful for churches that have identified an area of weakness and yet struggle to know how to address it. Identifying reasons why the network is weak, and/or why attempts to rectify the weakness have failed, can be a way of exploring deeper issues within church life.

Theological reflection can also be seen as a form of Christian discernment. Discernment asks the question, "What is God wanting me to do?," but also requires close attention to existing realities. Such reflection should not simply be left to academic theologians, but is the responsibility of all Christians. It is also something that can take place within community. Young people as well as adults can be drawn into the practice of discernment.

One model of theological reflection is known as the "pastoral cycle,"[9] and involves a process of describing the experience or situation, analyzing

8. On the need for disciples young and old to be reflective, see Walton, *Reflective Disciple*, esp. 111–42.

9. A helpful overview of the origins and development of the pastoral cycle, as well as

the problem, discerning God's will, and putting it into practice.[10] Engaging with the pastoral cycle can also be a means by which churches and young people can reflect on the eight networks of faith formation.

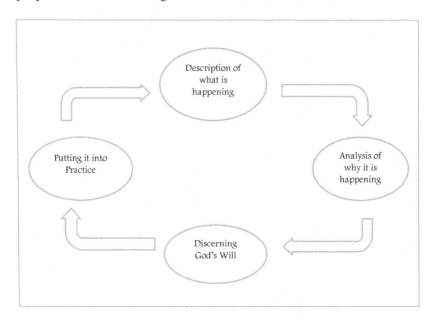

Diagram 1: The Pastoral Cycle

One example of the pastoral cycle at work is demonstrated at St. Stephens, a Methodist church in a rural English village. Steve coached the church over two and a half months as they reflected on their church and youth program, encouraging the church to work through the pastoral cycle.

At the initial stage, Steve explored with the church the question, "What's happening?" Steve met with a group of young people, adult youth volunteers, and church leaders, and together they identified the strengths and weaknesses of their program. Weaknesses included a lack parental involvement as well as a failure of the church to support parents in the spiritual nurturing of their teenagers and children. It seemed that the youth ministry was being outsourced to the youth worker and the team. While the church had previously identified these issues as problems, their attempt

---

its more recent variations, can be found in Thompson et al., *SCM Studyguide to Theological Reflection*, 51–61.

10. This is arguably more of a spiral rather than a cycle, since each new way of moving forward provokes new questions, and so the cycle begins again.

to resolve it had not met with success. Seeking to recruit parents and other church members to help with youth events had proved unsuccessful; parents simply said that they were too busy.

At the next stage, the church began to explore the question, "Why is this happening?" Those involved in the process looked beyond the local church context to broader cultural and social issues, and discovered that churches were not the only organizations that struggled to involve parents.[11] Church groups, Scouts, and sports teams all had problems recruiting adults to be involved in the lives of young people. It was clear from the research that adults felt it was important to be involved in the lives of young people, but there was a gap between this belief and actually volunteering. Other reasons included a culture of allowing professionals to work with the young people, habits of inaction, and heavy parental workloads.

The church also focused on its own role. Those involved in the process visited the parents of all the young people associated with the church, even the parents who did not attend the church themselves. At each visit, conversation focused on what the program was doing and its goals. Parents were asked what they thought and how they might want to be involved, as well as why they thought adults might be reluctant to participate. The church began to see obstacles that hindered adult involvement, and were encouraged to discover the good will that parents had towards the youth program.

In the third phase, the church focused on the question, "What is God's response?" They explored this question through engaging with Scripture and theology, encouraging all within the church to participate. Youth groups, home groups, and the leadership team engaged in Bible studies examining the interactive nature of all generations in Scripture. They also prayed for direction, calling for a joint church meeting to ask for God's guidance as they continued the process.

In the final phase, the church explored the question, "What is the best way forward?" This involved each small group coming up with ideas, and the church as a whole agreeing to practice new ways of being church. While the church had struggled to recruit parents to help with youth events, it began to offer more activities for families as a whole, and so tapped into the desire of parents to spend time with their kids. It also changed the way the youth group functioned: it began to meet three times each month rather than four, but the youth leader began to spend more time with smaller

---

11. See, for instance, Clary and Rhodes, *Mobilizing Adults for Positive Youth Development*.

groups of youth in the church, while also looking for ways to continue engagement with churched and non-churched parents.

Engaging in the pastoral cycle takes more time and effort than simply analyzing existing networks of faith formation. It can, however, be an invaluable tool for helping all within the church to identify key issues and to take ownership of the solution that emerges. It can also develop skills of theological reflection. Such a process empowers young people, as well as adults and leaders, to look at ministry with fresh eyes and find exciting ways to go forward.

EMPOWERING THE PEOPLE OF GOD

The networks for faith formation approach encourages all within the church to work together in nurturing faith—leaders, youth workers, parents, congregation members, and young people themselves. Each individual or group can be encouraged to consider relating to young people, and others too, as a key way in which to build up the church.

Church Leaders

The leader or leaders of the church have a particularly significant contribution. It is the leader who sets the spiritual culture and vision of a church. By their actions as well as their words, they indicate the priorities for the church, and set out the curriculum of faith formation for those who attend.

When church leaders marginalize or ignore the youth within their midst, youth are less likely to feel at home in the church. Similarly, when church leaders delegate all responsibility for youth to the youth worker, then youth will often see themselves as less important than other members of the church.

In a study of "Exemplary Congregations in Youth Ministry,"[12] the authors note that it is the congregational culture that is the most important factor in nurturing the faith of youth. That culture, however, receives its form and shape from the leaders within it. The leader's passion for God and young people sets the tone for the whole congregation, including the degree to which all within the church—young and old—are included.

---

12. See Martinson et al., *Spirit and Culture of Youth Ministry*. For a brief summary of the study, see Martinson and Black, "Special Research Report."

The leaders have a key role in helping young people engage in worship. Church leaders can arrange with those leading worship to ensure that young people are invited to participate fully. This might mean including prayers that reflect the concerns of teens as well as adults, or selecting songs that suit the culture of youth as well as the mature. Church leaders can also empower young people to help contribute in the leading of worship as well, since this is a key way to build up teenagers in the faith.

By virtue of their role and prominence in the church, the leader will also act as an informal mentor to many youth. As the research notes,

> Pastors influence young people, and the congregation, in ways they talk about God, pray, and ask for forgiveness when they hurt someone. Young people report that their pastors have a direct and profound impact on them spiritually and relationally.[13]

Leaders who take seriously networks for faith formation will create the culture and the opportunities for such networks to exist. As well as working with youth leaders and parent, and spending time with youth themselves, they can encourage all within the congregation to value and love the youth in their midst.

Youth Workers

While a networks for faith formation approach may seem to marginalize the role of the youth worker, youth workers can continue to play a key role within church. Research shows that churches that employ youth workers are far more likely to be growing churches,[14] and those churches that prioritize youth ministry are more likely to flourish.

It is also true, however, that youth workers have not stemmed the tide of church decline. Youth workers have spoken of the frustration of seeing strong Christian teenagers leave the faith when they leave school, and of doubting their own worth within it.[15] Youth workers also experience a great deal of pressure and stress in being identified as *the* person responsible for the youth of the church. In such a situation, many employed to work with

13. Martinson and Black, "Special Research Report," 53–54.

14. Brierley, *Reaching and Keeping Tweenagers*; Church Growth Research Programme, "From Anecdote to Evidence," 26.

15. See veteran youth worker (now sadly deceased) Mike Yaconelli's article, "The Failure of Youth Ministry." While published in 2003, similar concerns about youth ministry—at least in some of its models—continue to be raised.

youth wander from church to church, with only a minority remaining committed in the long-term to a single congregation.

In a networks for faith formation approach, the role of the youth workers becomes somewhat different. Rather than being responsible for the discipleship of young people, the youth worker becomes a bridge builder between young people and the rest of the congregation.[16] The role of the youth workers is primarily to create opportunities for young people to be exposed to networks of faith formation, such as through creating or nurturing intergenerational events and relationships, encouraging adults to mentor young people, equipping parents to model and teach faith within the home, and taking young people on missions and camps.

Youth workers will, of course, still run intentional events for young people, and spend time with young people in a way that many currently do. Youth workers should certainly see part of what they do as mentoring and teaching the youth that they serve. But the times spent with young people will be set within a context where a range of relationships exist between all within the church. The youth workers will not be possessive of the young people under their watch, but will rejoice when teenagers start meeting with other adults in the church, or when parents take a greater interest in the curriculum they have designed for their group.

Such an approach is supported by the Church of England's "Church Growth Research,"[17] as well as various US studies, which found that the best youth programs also built community within the church. Research on the intergenerational church similarly highlights the potential of the youth worker to be someone who can encourage relationships to be built across the church community.

Being an effective youth worker means empowering parents, the adult congregation, and even the local community to be involved with young people in order to create an interconnected network of support. What is important is not the number of young people that are present within a church ministry, but the depth of their discipleship that grows with the support of a thick cluster of relational networks.

---

16. Other writers in youth ministry make similar points. Dean and Foster, for example, encourage those working with youth to "share the mantle" with all within the church (*Godbearing Life*, 89–102).

17. Church Growth Research Programme, "From Anecdote to Evidence."

Parents

While parents are sometimes neglected in works of youth ministry, recent years have seen a flood of studies on the importance of parents in shaping faith. As demonstrated in chapter 4, parents play a key role in passing on faith to their children. Whatever else church leaders and youth workers do, they must help their parents realize their calling to raise their children "in the discipline and instruction of the Lord" (Eph 6:4b).

Parents also have a key role in introducing children to networks for faith formation, intentionally seeking out relationships and settings in which young people can grow. While encouraging regular attendance at church is important,[18] parents can also explore other ways that their children can engage, such as helping with the welcome team, playing in the band, and taking part in the small group.

Parents can also keep an eye on their child's friendship group, and can encourage opportunities for their kids to build relationships with Christian peers. They can similarly help link their children up with mentors, other Christian adults who can speak with wisdom and encouragement into their lives. While such relationships can sometime cause parents to feel jealous, they can be crucially important for the developing faith of teenagers.[19]

Family life as a whole can also be a reflection of gospel living, a community of the cross and resurrection that seeks in all its activities to reflect love of God and neighbor.[20] This is a high calling, but one that reminds parents that the call to faithfulness applies us much to their family life as it does to their church attendance.

Congregation Members

As we have emphasized throughout this book, the whole congregation has a key role to play in the life of young people. Young people, in fact, desire and long for relationships with their elders. Some adults have so often brought into the myth of the "rebellious youth" that they fear engaging them. But as one sixteen-year-old old female said in a research interview, "we want

---

18. As noted in chapter 4, helping kids stay engaged with the church, including through creating a family culture that regularly attends church, is key (Lytch, *Choosing Church*, 166–83.

19. Dean and Foster, *Godbearing Life*, 83–84.

20. Clapp, *Family at the Crossroads*, 146–49; McCarthy, *Good Life*, 49–57.

the adults to take an interest, to hear our stories, to support us and never ignore us."

In the Exemplary Youth Ministry Study in the US, the young people interviewed regularly spoke directly about qualities, relationships, and practices in the youth ministries of their congregations as critical to their life of faith. In the research, the youth indicated that the congregation had profoundly shaped both their life and their faith in specific and concrete ways. One young woman stated:

> I experience God at work in the lives my friends and our adults here; this church is the most real place in my life. I find hope and support for working out my life in a very difficult family situation. Without these people caring and praying for me, I don't know how I would make it. I live off the worship experiences and people here who believe in me.[21]

Congregations as a whole need to think about their children, teenagers, and emerging adults in every aspect of church life. This is the most teachable age and most conversions happen before the age of twenty-five. When a church thinks of evangelism and discipleship, it needs to start with its own young people. The most effective action a congregation can take for spiritual and numerical health is to create a culture where children and youth are a priority for all ages.

Every part of the church—from small groups to the finance committee—needs to ask how they can invest and support their young people. As the Church of England "Anecdote to Evidence" report argued, churches facing decline urgently need to focus on children, young people, and their parents, as well as investing in ways that help young people explore faith.[22]

Churches can also empower young people to be involved in the ministry and worship in the church, and church committees can seek their viewpoint and advice, including around issues such as worship and youth groups. Adults can provide a context where young people grow in their knowledge and experience of the faith.

Finally, simple and organic relationships between adults and youth within the congregation should be encouraged. To nurture such relationships, adults and youth need courage to step over the generational threshold that often separates them. The simple act of entering into conversation with another will be remembered, while serving alongside a young person

---

21. Martinson, "Spirit of Youth Ministry," 7.

22. Church Growth Research Programme, "From Anecdote to Evidence," 26.

in mission or ministry will also leave a mark. Teenagers will feel the love and support of the church when adults take an interest in them and pray for them.

Young People

While young people are often seen as passive recipients of the church's ministry, a networks for faith formation approach encourages them to be active in their faith, and particularly through engaging in a range of networks and relationships.

Such an approach encourages young people to seek spiritual support from peers, and reach out to older mentors too. It equips them to actively contribute to the ministry of the church, as well as engage in service and mission.

Young people can also be equipped to understand the role that they have in the lives of others.[23] As members of the body of Christ, they too are called to contribute to building up the church (Eph 4:12). This might mean helping to plan worship, serving on a mission team, encouraging others in the faith, and even mentoring adults![24]

Such an approach also means that young people need know their identity in Christ, the why and how of worship, and their own call to mission. Through the worship of the church and intentional faith formation, both young and old can grow into the "light of the knowledge of the glory of God in the face of Jesus Christ" (2 Cor 4:6).

Young people can also engage in theological reflection for themselves. They too can adopt the pastoral cycle, beginning with the issues and concerns that they face. A number of works can equip the church to help young people in this task, and such an approach can bring change to the church, the local community, and even the world.[25]

Youth are hardwired to explore and experiment, pursue ideas and challenge them too.[26] Their passion and energy can be embraced within a network approach, creating a context for the church to help them embrace

23. For importance of helping young people embrace their mission and vocation, see White, *Practicing Discernment*.

24. Crepes, *Reverse Mentoring*.

25. See White, *Practicing Discernment*; Clark and Powell, *Deep Ministry in a Shallow World*; Emery-Wright, *Empowering Young People*.

26. White, *Practicing Discernment*, 23.

their vocation as young people. As they do so, they too will grow in holiness and witness the Spirit at work in their midst.

CONCLUSION

Networks for faith formation can be a practical framework for helping churches support young people in their midst. Such an approach adopts a holistic approach to faith formation, one that takes seriously the ecology of relationships that shapes young people.

While helping young people grow in faith requires a number of networks, those working with youth also need to think carefully about the theology that young people are taught, the ecclesiology that nurtures them, and the missional approach that they are encouraged to adopt. Churches will differ on how they approach such issues, but addressing them is crucial.[27]

Networks for faith formation are also wholly insufficient if separated from the work of the Spirit, or if considered as a semi-Pelagian attempt to shape youth apart from the grace of God. While the social sciences reveal that a cluster of such networks give teenagers the best chance of owning faith for themselves and leading a holy life, faith are holiness are ultimately gifts of God, fanned into flame by the Spirit's work of grace. We are called to pray as well as to work.

When churches and Christians genuinely engage with the youth in their midst, they discover that not only young people mature in their faith, but that all ages benefit from a deepening relationships with God and each other. They demonstrate that the "faith that was once for all entrusted to the saints" (Jude 3) is for the young as well as the old, babes as well as elders in Christ. People of every age are called to grow in faith, passing on the praises of God to the next generation. As the psalmist puts it,

> We will tell the coming generation
> the glorious deeds of the LORD, and his might,
> and the wonders that he has done.
> (Ps 78:4b)

---

27. A networks approach to faith formation would not by itself prevent, for example, a drift into Moralistic Therapeutic Deism. Theology remains crucial in all discussions of church and mission.

Youth and the Online World: Five Principles

IN A BOOK ON networks for faith formation, it would be odd to avoid addressing the issue of the online world and the role that social (or virtual) networks play in the lives of young people.

The difficulty of addressing the subject is that the issues it raises are so vast that it would be impossible, in a brief appendix at least, to do any sort of justice to the complexities involved. The rate of change in the area is also so rapid that any discussion of a *particular* form of social media is likely to be out of date within just a few years.

Our own view is that online world, and particularly social media, can be used for good or for ill, and can help or hinder a young person's growth in faith. Rather than offering a detailed discussion, we offer here *five principles* for helping churches approach this issue. Our hope is that these can prompt reflection and discussion of how best to engage in this area, and provide at least some guidance for parents in particular.

1. SOCIAL NETWORKS ARE HUGELY INFLUENTIAL FOR YOUTH.

A Pew research report in 2015 found that 92 percent of US teens went online daily, with 24 percent of teens saying that they were online "almost constantly."[1] Newspaper articles from across the world frequently point

1. Lenhart, "Teens, Social Media & Technology."

to the popularity of social media sites, often highlighting their negative effects.[2]

Given the influence of social networks today, Christian parents, as well as youth leaders, need to become aware of the benefits and risks of online engagement, and be aware how it can shape and influence a young person's values and faith.

2. PARENTS NEED TO MODEL HEALTHY WAYS OF ENGAGING THE ONLINE WORLD.

While some adults allow young people to engage online without any guidance at all, others restrict online activity to the very minimum. Research suggests that both strategies are unhelpful.[3] Instead, parents should actively guide their children online, acting as "digital mentors."[4]

Just as children learn from parents and adults in other areas of life, parents can model wisdom in online engagement provide helpful guidance for their children. While teenagers will likely spend more time online without supervision, parents can keep the conversations with them open and remain engaged with how their children interact on social media.

3. PARENTS AND CHURCHES NEED TO HELP YOUNG PEOPLE GUARD AGAINST THE NEGATIVE ASPECTS OF THE ONLINE WORLD.

The online world can be a dangerous and destructive place. Young people can be bullied and intimidated, shaped by images of beauty that lead to self-hate, and exposed to pornography. While such negative possibilities can be overestimated, they must not be taken lightly.

Parents in particular need to be guard their children against the negative dimensions of the online world, including as they grow into the teenage years. Exposure to pornography can be particularly damaging,[5] with some research claiming that nine out of ten boys and six out of ten girls have

2. For a British example, see Weale, "Teens' Night-Time Use."

3. See the helpful discussion of "three patterns of digital parenting", summarizing research by Alexandra Samuel, in Kehrwald et al., *Families at the Center*, 40–41.

4. Ibid., 41.

5. For the harmful ways in which pornography can "hijack" the male brain, see Struthers, *Wired for Intimacy*.

seen online pornography before the age of eighteen.[6] Parents may consider blocking or filtering software on computers and phones to prevent young people accessing such material, while teenagers seeking help in this area will need the support of a variety of networks.[7]

4. PARENTS AND CHURCHES NEED TO HELP YOUNG PEOPLE ENGAGE POSITIVELY WITH THE ONLINE WORLD.

The online world can be a wonderful and stimulating place. Young people can build new relationships, strengthen existing ones, and explore ideas and experiences in a way that would have been impossible just a couple of generations ago. Churches can celebrate the many gifts of information, relationships, and knowledge that the online world brings.

Given the presence of young people on social media, it is also important that other Christians are present with them and encourage them through that medium. While this does not meant that every parent or church leader needs to engage, this could be one way in which a youth minister remains present to the young people they serve.

5. TIME AWAY FROM SOCIAL NETWORKS IS IMPORTANT.

The work of Sherry Turkle has demonstrated that too much time online damages the ability of young people to relate socially,[8] and other research similar points to the negative effects of excessive screen time (whether on phones, computers, or TV screens). Other thinkers point out the ways in which social media can shape us in damaging ways, including around our views of the self.[9]

It is important, then, for parents to ensure their children spend significant periods of time offline, and to be positive role models for them too. This might involve agreeing on a "no screens" rule during meal times, or

6. See Frad, "10 Shocking Statistics," who also notes that 71 percent of teens have also attempted to hide their online activity from parents.

7. On the importance of giving young people information and guidance on sexuality in general, see Emery-Wright, *Understanding Teenage Sexuality.*

8. Turkle, *Alone Together* and *Reclaiming Conversation.*

9. Smith, *Imagining the Kingdom,* 143–45.

perhaps designating Sunday as a digital Sabbath for the family. Such ways of regulating the use of screens in the family are going to become increasingly important as technology continues to develop.

RECOMMENDED READING

Detweiler, Craig. *iGods: How Technology Shapes Our Spiritual and Social Lives*. Grand Rapids: Baker, 2013.

Detweiler offers a detailed analysis of the ways in which technologies shape us while also offering wisdom and guidance for Christians thinking about how best to engage with the online world.

Lewis, Bex. *Raising Children in a Digital Age: Enjoying the Best, Avoiding the Worst*. Oxford: Lion Hudson, 2014.

Since it is good to start early with children, Lewis's work offers a helpful exploration of the positives of online engagement while also helping parents guard against the negatives.

Powell, Kara, et al. *Right Click: Parenting Your Teenager in a Digital Media World*. Pasadena, CA: Fuller Youth Institute, 2015.

A helpful and accessible book that helps parents support and guide their teenage children in a world of digital media. The authors encourage parents to avoid negativity and instead enter into conversations with their children about technology and its use.

Bibliography

Adamczyk, Amy, and Jacob Felson. "Friends' Religiosity and First Sex." *Social Science Research* 35 (2006) 924–47.

Aisthorpe, Steve. *The Invisible Church: Learning from the Experiences of Churchless Christians.* Edinburgh: Saint Andrew, 2016.

Allen, Holly Catterton, and Christine Lawton Ross. *Intergenerational Christian Formation.* Downers Grove, IL: IVP Academic, 2012.

American Camp Association. "Inspirations: Developmental Supports and Opportunities of Youths' Experiences at Camp." 2006. http://www.acacamps.org/sites/default/files/resource_library/Inspirations.pdf.

Anderson, Bernhard W. *The Living World of the Old Testament.* 4th ed. Essex: Longman, 1988.

Anderson, Keith R., and Randy D. Reese. *Spiritual Mentoring: A Guide for Seeking and Giving Direction.* Downers Grove, IL: InterVarsity, 1999.

Anglican Communion. "Marks of Mission." http://www.anglicancommunion.org/identity/marks-of-mission.aspx.

Anthony, Michael, and Michelle Anthony, eds. *A Theology for Family Ministries.* Nashville: B&H Academic, 2011.

Atkinson, Harley T., and Joel Comiskey. "Lessons from the Early House Church for Today's Cell Group." *Christian Education Journal*, series 3, 11/1 (2014) 75–87.

Augustine. *Confessions.* Translated by Henry Chadwick. Oxford: Oxford University Press, 1991.

Bader, Christopher D., and Scott A. Desmond. "Do as I Say and as I Do: The Effects of Consistent Parental Beliefs and Behaviors upon Religious Transmission." *Sociology of Religion* 67/3 (2006) 313–29.

Bakke, O. M. *When Children Became People: The Birth of Childhood in Early Christianity.* Minneapolis: Augsburg Fortress, 2005.

Banks, Robert. *Paul's Idea of Community.* Rev. ed. Peabody, MA: Hendrickson, 1994.

Barna Group. "5 Reason Millennials Stay Connected to the Church." September 2013. https://www.barna.org/barna-update/millennials/635-5-reasons-millennials-stay-connected-to-church.html#.VriIR_mLSUk.

Bibliography

―――. "State of the Bible 2015: Teens." 2013. http://www.americanbible.org/uploads/content/Teens_State_of_the_Bible_2015_Report.pdf.

Barry, C. M., and K. R. Wentzel. "Friend Influence on Prosocial Behavior: The Role of Motivational Factors and Friendship Characteristics." *Developmental Psychology* 41 (2006) 153–63.

Barth, Karl. *Church Dogmatics.* IV.I: *The Doctrine of Reconciliation.* Edinburgh: T. & T. Clark, 1956.

Bauckham, Richard. *God Crucified: Monotheism and Christology in the New Testament.* Carlisle: Paternoster, 1998.

Bauman, Zygmunt *Liquid Life.* Cambridge, UK: Polity, 2005.

―――. *Liquid Times: Living in an Age of Uncertainty.* Cambridge, UK: Polity, 2007.

Beale, Gregory K. "Eden, the Temple, and the Church's Mission." *Journal of the Evangelical Theological Society* 48/1 (2005) 5–31.

―――. *A New Testament Biblical Theology: The Unfolding of the Old Testament in the New.* Grand Rapids: Baker Academic, 2011.

―――. *The Temple and the Church's Mission: A Biblical Theology of the Dwelling Place of God.* Downers Grove, IL: InterVarsity, 2004.

Bengtson, Vern L., with Norella M. Putney and Susan Harris. *Families and Faith: How Religion Is Passed Down Across Generations.* Oxford: Oxford University Press, 2013.

Berman, Steve L., et al. "Identity Exploration, Commitment, and Distress: A Cross-National Investigation in China, Taiwan, Japan, and the United States." *Child and Youth Care Forum* 40 (2011) 65–75.

Bonhoeffer, Dietrich. *Life Together.* Translated by John W. Doberstein. New York: Harper & Row, 1954.

Bosch, David J. "Evangelism: Theological Currents and Cross-Currents Today." *International Bulletin of Missionary Research* (1987) 98–103.

―――. *Transforming Mission: Paradigm Shifts in Theology of Mission.* Maryknoll, NY: Orbis, 1996.

Bowers, Edmond B., et al. *Promoting Positive Youth Development: Lessons from the 4-H Study.* Switzerland: Springer International, 2015.

Brierley, Peter. *Reaching and Keeping Tweenagers.* London: Christian Research, 2002.

Brown, Colin, ed. *The New International Dictionary of New Testament Theology.* Vol. 2. Exeter: Paternoster, 1976.

Bunge, Marcia J., ed. *The Child in the Bible.* Grand Rapids: Eerdmans, 2008

Bunton, Peter. "300 Years of Small Groups—The European Church from Luther to Wesley." *Christian Education Journal,* series 3, 11/1 (2014), 88–106.

Cameron, Helen. *Resourcing Mission: Practical Theology for Changing Churches.* London: SCM, 2010.

Cardoza-Orlandi, Carlos F. *Mission: An Essential Guide.* Nashville: Abingdon, 2002.

Centre for Addiction and Mental Health. "Youth Mentoring Linked to Many Positive Effects, New Study Shows." *ScienceDaily,* January 2013. http://www.sciencedaily.com/releases/2013/01/130115143850.htm.

Christie, Lee. *Unfinished Sentences: 450 Tantalizing Statement-Starters to Get Teenagers Talking and Thinking.* Grand Rapids: Zondervan, 2000.

Church Growth Research Programme. "From Anecdote to Evidence: Findings from the Church Growth Research Programme 2011–2013." 2014. http://www.churchgrowthresearch.org.uk/UserFiles/File/Reports/FromAnecdoteToEvidence1.0.pdf.

Bibliography

Clark, Chap. *Hurt 2.0: Inside the World of Today's Teenagers.* Grand Rapids: Baker Academic, 2011.

————, ed. *Youth Ministry in the 21st Century: Five Views.* Grand Rapids: BakerAcademic, 2015.

Clark, Chap, and Kara E. Powell. *Deep Justice in a Broken World: Helping Your Kids Serve Others and Right the Wrongs around Them.* Grand Rapids: Zondervan, 2007.

————. *Deep Ministry in a Shallow World: Not-So-Secret Findings about Youth Ministry.* Grand Rapids: Zondervan, 2006.

Clapp, Rodney, *Family at the Crossroads: Beyond Traditional and Modern Options.* Downers Grove, IL: InterVarsity, 1993.

Clapper, Gregory S. *The Renewal of the Heart Is the Mission of the Church: Wesley's Heart Religion in the Twenty-First Century.* Cambridge, UK: Lutterworth, 2011.

Clary, E. Gil, and Jean E. Rhodes. *Mobilizing Adults for Positive Youth Development: Strategies for Closing the Gap between Beliefs and Behaviors.* New York: Springer Science+Business, 2006.

Commission on Children at Risk. *Hardwired to Connect: The New Scientific Case for Authoritative Communities.* Institute for American Values, 2003. http://www.americanvalues.org/search/item.php?id=17.

Cortez, Marc. *Theological Anthropology: A Guide for the Perplexed.* London: T. & T. Clark, 2010.

Collins-Mayo, Sylvia, et al. *The Faith of Generation Y.* London: Church Publishing, 2010.

Creps, Earl. *Reverse Mentoring: How Young Leaders Can Transform the Church and Why We Should Let Them.* SanFrancisco: Jossey-Bass, 2008.

Dean, Kenda Creasy. *Almost Christian: What the Faith of Our Teenagers Is Telling the American Church.* Oxford: Oxford University Press, 2010.

————. *Practicing Passion: Youth and the Quest for a Passionate Church.* Grand Rapids: Eerdmans, 2004.

Dean, Kenda Creasy, and Ron Foster. *The Godbearing Life: The Art of Soul Tending for Youth Ministry.* Nashville: Upper Room, 1998.

DeBois, David L., et al. "How Effective Are Mentoring Programs for Youth? A Systematic Assessment of the Evidence." *Psychological Sciences in the Public Interest* 12/2 (2011) 57–91.

Detweiler, Craig. *iGods. How Technology Shapes Our Spiritual and Social Lives.* Grand Rapids: Baker, 2013.

DeVries, Mark. *Family-Based Youth Ministry.* Rev. ed. Downers Grove, IL: InterVarsity, 2004.

DeYoung, Kevin, and Greg Gilbert. *What Is the Mission of the Church?: Making Sense of Social Justice, Shalom, and the Great Commission.* Wheaton, IL: Crossway, 2011.

Donahue, Bill, and Charles Gowler. "Small Groups: The Same Yesterday, Today, and Forever?" *Christian Education Journal*, series 3, 11/1 (2014) 118–33.

Dougherty, Kevin D., and Andrew L. Whitehead. "A Place to Belong: Small Group Involvement in Religious Congregations." *Sociology of Religion* 72/1 (2011) 91–111.

Dumbrell, W. J. *Covenant and Creation: A Theology of the Old Testament Covenants.* Carlisle: Paternoster, 1984.

Dunn, James D. G. *The Parting of the Ways between Christianity and Judaism and Their Significance for the Character of Christianity.* 2nd ed. London: SCM, 2006.

Edie, Fred P. *Book, Bath, Table, and Time: Christian Worship as Source and Resource for Youth Ministry.* Cleveland: Pilgrim, 2007.

Egeler, Daniel. *Mentoring Millennials: Shaping the Next Generation.* Colorado Springs, CO: NavPress, 2003.

Eisner, Elliot W. *The Educational Imagination: On the Design and Evaluation of School Programs.* New York: Macmillan, 1985.

Elkind, David. *A Sympathetic Understanding of the Child: Birth to Sixteen.* Boston: Allyn and Bacon, 1994.

Emery-Wright, Steve. *Empowering Young People in Church.* Cambridge, UK: Grove, 2008.

———. *Now That Was Worship.* Calver, Derbyshire: Cliff College, 2012.

———. "A Study of Liminality for the Purpose of Transformation." *Journal of Youth and Theology* 12/2 (2014) 40–54.

———. *Understanding Teenage Sexuality: A Foundation for Christian Relationships.* Singapore: Armour, 2009.

Erikson, Erik H. *Identity, Youth and Crisis.* London: Faber, 1968.

Ferdinando, Keith. "Mission: A Problem of Definition." *Themelios* 33/1 (2008) 46–59.

Ferguson, Everett. *Backgrounds of Early Christianity.* 2nd ed. Grand Rapids: Eerdmans, 1993.

———. *The Church of Christ: A Biblical Ecclesiology for Today.* Grand Rapids: Eerdmans, 1996.

Field, Clive D. "Bible Literacy and Other News." British Religion in Numbers, February 2014. http://www.brin.ac.uk/2014/bible-literacy-and-other-news.

Fiske, Susan T. *Social Beings: Core Motives in Social Psychology.* 2nd ed. London: Wiley, 2010.

Flavel, John. *Keeping the Heart: How to Maintain Your Love for God.* Lake Wyle, SC: Christian Heritage, 2012.

Fleischer, Barbara J. "Mezirow's Theory of Transformative Learning and Lonergan's Method in Theology: Resources for Adult Theological Education." *Journal of Adult Theological Education* 3/2 (2006) 147–62.

Foster, Charles R. *From Generation to Generation: The Adaptive Challenge of Mainline Protestant Education in Forming Faith.* Eugene, OR: Cascade, 2012.

Foster, Richard J. *Celebration of Discipline: The Path to Spiritual Growth, rev. ed.* London: Hodder & Stoughton, 1989.

———. *Streams of Living Water.* San Francisco: Harper & Row, 1998.

Frad, Matt. "10 Shocking Stats about Teens and Pornography." Covenant Eyes, April 2015. http://www.covenanteyes.com/2015/04/10/10-shocking-stats-about-teens-and-pornography.

Francis, Leslie J. "Implicit Religion, Explicit Religion and Purpose in Life: An Empirical Enquiry among 13 to 15 Year-Old Adolescents." *Mental Health, Religion & Culture* 16/9 (2013) 909–21.

Francis, Leslie J., and Thomas E. Evans. "Insights from Scholarship: The Relationship between Personal Prayer and Purpose in Life among Churchgoing and Non-churchgoing Twelve-to-Fifteen-Year-Olds in the UK." *Religious Education* 91/1 (1996) 8–21.

Francis, Leslie J., and Mandy Robbins. *Urban Hope and Spiritual Health: The Adolescent Voice.* Peterborough: Epworth, 2005.

Frazee, Randy. *The Connecting Church: Beyond Small Groups to Authentic Community.* Grand Rapids: Zondervan, 2001.

Fretheim, Terrence E. *God and World in the Old Testament: A Relational Theology of Creation.* Nashville: Abingdon, 2005.

Frost, Andy. *Losing Faith.* Milton Keynes: Authentic Media, 2010.

Bibliography

Garland, Diana R. *Family Ministry: A Comprehensive Guide.* 2nd ed. Downers Grove, IL: InterVarsity, 2012.

Gardner, Jason. *Mend the Gap: Can the Church Reconnect the Generations?* Nottingham: InterVarsity, 2008.

Gentry, Peter J., and Stephen J. Wellum. *God's Kingdom through God's Covenants: A Concise Biblical Theology.* Wheaton, IL: Crossway, 2015.

Gill, Robin. *Churchgoing and Christian Ethics.* Cambridge, UK: Cambridge University Press, 1999.

Goheen, Michael W. *A Light to the Nations: The Missional Church and the Biblical Story.* Grand Rapids: Baker Academic, 2011.

Greenberger, Ellen, Chuansheng Chen, and Margaret R. Beam. "The Role of 'Very Important' Nonparental Adults in Adolescent Development." *Journal of Youth and Adolescence* 27/3 (1998) 321–43.

Grenz, Stanley J. *Sexual Ethics: An Evangelical Perspective.* Louisville: Westminster John Knox, 1990.

———. *Theology for the Community of God.* Carlisle: Paternoster, 1994.

Hafemann, Scot J., and Paul R. House, eds. *Central Themes in Biblical Theology: Mapping Unity in Diversity.* Nottingham: Apollos, 2007.

Hamilton, Victor P. *The Book of Genesis, Chapters 1–17.* Grand Rapids: Eerdmans., 1990.

Haskell, D. Millard, and Kevin N. Flatt. "When Youth Experience God: The Reported Impact of a Mainline Protestant Youth Rally and a Charismatic-Evangelical Youth Rally on Attendee's Religious Faith." *Journal of Youth Ministry* 13/2 (2015) 21–52.

Hawkins, Greg L., and Cally Parkinson. *Move: What 1,000 Churches Reveal about Spiritual Growth.* Grand Rapids: Zondervan, 2011.

Hays, Richard B. *Reading Backwards: Figural Christology and the Fourfold Gospel Witness.* London: SPCK, 2015.

Heflin, Houstin. *Youth Pastor: The Theology and Practice of Youth Ministry.* Nashville: Abingdon, 2009.

Hellerman, J. H. *When the Church Was a Family: Recapturing Jesus' Vision for Authentic Christian Community.* Nashville: B&H Academic, 2009.

Holmes, Michael W., ed. *The Apostolic Fathers: Greek Texts and English Translations.* Rev. ed. Grand Rapids: Baker, 1999.

Hope Together. "Hope in Our Villages and Towns." http://www.hopetogether.org.uk.

Horton, Michael. *The Christian Faith: A Systematic Theology for Pilgrims on the Way.* Grand Rapids: Zondervan, 2011.

Howell, Brian M. "Mission to Nowhere: Putting Short-Term Missions into Context." *International Bulletin of Missionary Research* 33/4 (2009) 206–11.

Howell, Brian M., et al. "Should Churches Abandon Travel-Intensive Short-Term Missions in Favor of Local Projects?" *Christianity Today*, June 2012. http://www.christianitytoday.com/ct/2012/june/short-term-missions.html.

Icenogle, Gareth Weldon. *Biblical Foundations for Small Group Ministry.* Downers Grove, IL: InterVarsity, 1994.

Inge, John *A Christian Theology of Place.* Aldershot: Ashgate, 2003.

Jacober, Amy E. *The Adolescent Journey: An Interdisciplinary Approach.* Downers Grove, IL: InterVarsity, 2011.

Jindra, Ines. *A New Model of Religious Conversion.* Leiden: Brill, 2014.

Johnson, Luke Timothy. "Making Connections: The Material Expression of Friendship in the New Testament." *Interpretation* 58/2 (2004) 158–71.

BIBLIOGRAPHY

Johnson, W. Brad, and Charles R. Ridley. *The Elements of Mentoring.* Rev. ed. London: Palgrave Macmillan, 2004.

Jones, Andrew. *Pilgrimage: The Journey to Remembering Our Story.* Abingdon: BRF, 2011.

Jones, Brian. "Why Churches Should Euthanize Small Groups." *Christian Standard,* January 2011.http://christianstandard.com/2011/01/why-churches-should-euthanize-small-groups.

Jones, L. Gregory. "Discovering Hope Through Holy Friendships." *Faith and Leadership,* June 2012. https://www.faithandleadership.com/l-gregory-jones-discovering-hope-through-holy-friendships.

Jones, Randall M., et al. "Friendship Characteristics, Psychosocial Development, and Adolescent Identity Formation." *Personal Relationships* 21 (2014) 51–67.

Jones, Tony. *The Sacred Way: Spiritual Practices for Everyday Life.* Grand Rapids: Zondervan, 2005.

Kehrwald, Leif, et al. *Families at the Center of Faith Formation.* Naugatuck, CT: LifelongFaith, 2016.

Keller, Tim. *Generous Justice: How God's Grace Makes Us Just.* New York: Dutton, 2010.

———. *Prayer: Experiencing Awe and Intimacy with God.* London: Hodder & Stoughton, 2014.

Kierkegaard, Søren. *Purity of Heart Is to Will One Thing: Spiritual Preparation for the Office of Confession.* Translated by Douglas V. Steere. New York: Harper & Row, 1938.

Kinnaman, David. *You Lost Me: Why Young Christians Are Leaving Church and Rethinking Faith.* Grand Rapids: Baker, 2011.

Knabb, Joshua J., and Joseph Pellitier. "'A Cord of Three Strands Is Not Easily Broken': An Empirical Investigation of Attachment-Based Small Group Functioning in the Christian Church." *Journal of Psychology & Theology* 42/4 (2014) 343–58.

Kruger, Michael J. *Canon Revisited: Establishing the Origins and Authority of the New Testament Books.* Wheaton, IL: Crossway, 2012.

Laing, Mark. "*Missio Dei:* Some Implications for the Church." *Missiology* 37/1 (2009) 89–91.

Lancaster University. "Why 'No Religion' Is the New Religion." January 2016. http://www.lancaster.ac.uk/news/articles/2016/why-no-religion-is-the-new-religion/.

Lanker, Jason. "The Family of Faith: The Place of Natural Mentoring in the Church's Christian Formation of Adolescents." *Christian Education Journal,* series 3, 2 (2010) 267–80.

———. "Life-Long Guides: The Role and Relationships of Natural Mentors in the Lives of Christian Adolescents." *Journal of Youth Ministry* 11/1 (2012) 31–43.

Lanker, Jason, and Klauss Issler. "The Relationship between Natural Mentoring and Spirituality." *Journal of Youth Ministry* 9/1 (2010) 93–109.

Lausanne Movement. "The Lausanne Covenant." https://www.lausanne.org/content/covenant/lausanne-covenant.

Lenhart, Amanda. "Teens, Social Media & Technology: Overview 2015." Pew Research Center, April 2015.http://www.pewinternet.org/2015/04/09/teens-social-media-technology-2015.

Lewis, Bex. *Raising Children in a Digital Age: Enjoying the Best, Avoiding the Worst.* Oxford: Lion Hudson, 2014.

Lewis, C. S. *The Four Loves.* London: HarperCollins, 1960.

Lewis, Rick. *Mentoring Matters.* Oxford: Monarch, 2009.

Lincoln, Sian. "'Feeling the Noise:' Teenagers, Bedrooms and Music." *Leisure Studies* 24 (2005) 399–414.

Bibliography

————. "'I've Stamped My Personality All Over It:' The Meaning of Objects in Teenage Bedroom Space." *Space and Culture* 17 (2014) 266–79.

Livermore, David A. *Cultural Intelligence: Improving your CQ to Engage Our Multicultural World*. Grand Rapids: Baker, 2009.

————. *Serving With Eyes Wide Open*. Grand Rapids: Baker, 2006.

Lytch, Carol Eichling. *Choosing Church: What Makes a Difference for Teens*. Louisville: Westminster John Knox, 2004.

Mackenzie, Ed. "Following Jesus in a Spiritual Age: Post-Religious Spirituality and the Letter to the Ephesians." *Evangelical Quarterly* 87/2 (2015) 137–50.

Mackenzie, Ed, and Gareth Crispin. *Together with God: An Introduction to Family Worship*. Birmingham, UK: Morse-Brown, 2016.

Mahan, Brian, et al., *Awakening Youth Discipleship: Christian Resistance in a Consumer Culture*. Eugene, OR: Cascade, 2008.

Mark, Olwyn. *Passing on Faith*. London: Theos, 2016. http://www.theosthinktank.co.uk/files/files/Reports/Passing%20on%20faith%20combined%20(1).pdf.

Martin, Todd F., et al. "Religious Socialization: A Test of the Channeling Hypothesis of Parental Influence on Adolescent Faith Maturity." *Journal of Adolescent Research* 18/2 (2003) 169–87.

Martinson, Roland. "The Spirit of Youth Ministry: A Study of Congregations with Youth of Vital Faith." Session One: Research Project Overview. http://www.firstthird.org/eym/Spirit-and-Culture-of-YM.pdf.

Martinson, Roland, and Wesley Black. "Special Research Report: The Spirit and Culture of Youth Ministry." *Lifelong Faith* 3/4 (2009) 38–60.

Martinson, Roland, Wesley Black, and John Roberto. *The Spirit and Culture of Youth Ministry: Leading Congregations toward Exemplary Youth Ministry*. St. Paul: EYM, 2010.

Mayo, Jeanne. *Thriving Youth Groups: Secrets for Growing Your Ministry*. Loveland, CO: Youthsource, 2005.

McCabe, Scott. "Who Needs a Holiday? Evaluating Social Tourism." *Annals of Tourism Research* 36/5 (2009) 667–88.

McCarthy, David Matzko. *The Good Life: Genuine Christianity for the Middle Class*. Grand Rapids: Brazos, 2004.

McConnell, Scott. "LifeWay Research Finds Reasons 18-to-22-Year-Olds Drop Out of Church." August 2007. http://www.lifeway.com/Article/LifeWay-Research-finds-reasons-18-to-22-year-olds-drop-out-of-church.

McKnight, Scot. *A Fellowship of Differents*. Grand Rapids: Zondervan, 2014.

Mezirow, Jack, and Associates. *Learning as Transformation: Critical Perspectives on a Theory in Progress*. San Francisco: Jossey-Bass, 2000.

Middleton, J. Richard. *The Liberating Image: The Imago Dei in Genesis 1*. Grand Rapids: Brazos, 2005.

Minear, Paul S. *Images of the Church in the New Testament*. Louisville: Westminster John Knox, 2004.

Montgomery, Alice, and Leslie J. Francis. "Relationship between Personal Prayer and School-Related Attitudes among 11–16-Year-Old Girls." *Psychological Reports* 78/3 (1996) 787–93.

Murphy, Debra Dean. *Teaching that Transforms: Worship at the Heart of Christian Education*. Grand Rapids: Brazos, 2004.

Nash, Sally, and Jo Whitehead, eds. *Christian Youth Work in Theory and Practice: A Handbook*. London: SCM, 2014.

BIBLIOGRAPHY

Newbigin, Lesslie. *The Open Secret: Sketches for a Missionary Theology*. Grand Rapids: Eerdmans, 1978.

Newby, Vicki, ed. *Camps, Retreats, Missions, & Service Ideas for Youth Groups*. Grand Rapids: Zondervan, 1997.

Newport, Frank. "Frequent Church Attendance Highest in Utah, Lowest in Vermont." Gallup, February 17, 2015. http://www.gallup.com/poll/181601/frequent-church-attendance-highest-utah-lowest-vermont.aspx.

Nooney, Jennifer G. "Religion, Stress, and Mental Health in Adolescence: Findings from Add Health." *Review of Religious Research* 46/4 (2005) 341–54.

Oden, Thomas C. *Classic Christianity. A Systematic Theology*. ePub ed. New York: HarperCollins, 2009.

Oestreicher, Jeannie, and Larry Warner. *Imaginative Prayer for Youth Ministry*. Grand Rapids: Zondervan, 2006.

Osiek, Carolyn, and David L. Bach. *Families in the New Testament World: Households and House Churches*. Louisville: Westminster John Knox, 1997

Owen, John. *Communion with the Triune God*. Edited by Kelly M. Kapic and Justin Taylor. Wheaton, IL: Crossway, 2007.

Packer, J. I., and Gary A. Parrett. *Grounded in the Gospel: Building Believers the Old-Fashioned Way*. Grand Rapids: Baker, 2010.

Peterson, Eugene H. *Practise Resurrection: A Conversation on Growing up in Christ*. London: Hodder & Stoughton, 2010.

Powell, Kara E., et al. *Right Click: Parenting your Teenager in a Digital Media World*. Pasadena, CA: Fuller Youth Institute, 2015.

Powell, Kara E., and Chap Clark. *Sticky Faith: Everyday Ideas to Build Lasting Faith in Your Kids*. Grand Rapids: Zondervan, 2011.

Priest, Robert J., and Joseph Paul Priest. "'They See Everything, and Understand Nothing': Short-Term Mission and Service Learning." *Missiology* 36/1 (2008) 53–73.

Rainbow, Paul. *Johannine Theology: The Gospel, the Epistles, and the Apocalypse*. Downers Grove, IL: InterVarsity, 2014.

Rappaport, Roy A. *Ritual and Religion in the Making of Humanity*. Cambridge, UK: Cambridge University Press, 1999.

Regnerus, Mark D. *Forbidden Fruit: Sex and Religion in the Lives of American Teenagers*. Oxford: Oxford University Press, 2007.

Renovaré. "Training over Trying." https://renovare.org.

Richter, Philip, and Leslie J. Francis. *Gone but Not Forgotten: Church Leaving and Returning*. London: Darton, Longman & Todd, 1998.

Root, Andrew. *Revisiting Relational Youth Ministry: From a Strategy of Influence to a Theology of Incarnation*. Downers Grove, IL: InterVarsity, 2007.

———. *Unlocking Mission and Eschatology in Youth Ministry*. Grand Rapids: Zondervan, 2012.

Routledge, Robin. *Old Testament Theology: A Thematic Approach*. Nottingham: Apollos, 2008.

Runyon, Theodore. *The New Creation: John Wesley's Theology Today*. Nashville: Abingdon, 1998.

Sandell, Jillian. "I'll Be There for You: Friends and the Fantasy of Alternative Families." *American Studies* 39/2 (1998) 141–55.

Sanders, Fred. *Wesley on the Christian Life: The Heart Renewed in Love*. Wheaton, IL: Crossway, 2013.

BIBLIOGRAPHY

Savage, Sara, et al. *Making Sense of Generation Y: The World View of 15 to 25-Year-Olds.* London: Church House, 2011.

Schnabel, Eckhard J. *Early Christian Mission.* 2 vols. Downers Grove, IL: InterVarsity, 2004.

Schnase, Robert. *Five Practices of Fruitful Congregations.* Nashville: Abingdon, 2007.

Schreiner, Thomas. *Faith Alone—The Doctrine of Justification.* Grand Rapids: Zondervan, 2015.

Schweitzer, Frank, et al., eds. *Youth, Religion and Confirmation Work in Europe: The Second Study.* Munich: Gütersloher, 2015.

Segal, Alan F. *Paul the Convert: The Apostolate and Apostasy of Saul the Pharisee.* New Haven, CT: Yale University Press, 1990.

Sheer, Michael, et al. "The Role of Community Service in the Faith Development of Adolescents." *Journal of Youth Ministry* 6/1 (2007) 43–54.

Shepherd, Nick. *Faith Generation: Retaining Young People and Growing the Church.* London: SPCK, 2016.

Sipe, Cynthia. "Mentoring Programs for Adolescents: A Research Summary." *Journal of Adolescent Health* 31 (2002) 251–60.

Smalley, Stephen S. *John: Evangelist and Interpreter.* Exeter: Paternoster, 1978.

Smith, Christian, with Melinda Lundquist Denton. *Soul Searching: The Religious and Spiritual Lives of American Teenagers.* Oxford: Oxford University Press, 2005.

Smith, Christian, with Patricia Snell. *Souls in Transition: The Religious and Spiritual Lives of Emerging Adults.* Oxford: Oxford University Press, 2009.

Smith, Gordon T. *Called to Be Saints: An Invitation to Christian Maturity.* Downers Grove, IL: InterVarsity, 2014.

Smith, James K. A. *Desiring the Kingdom: Worship, Worldview, and Cultural Formation.* Grand Rapids: Baker Academic, 2009.

———. *Imagining the Kingdom: How Worship Works.* Grand Rapids: Baker Academic, 2013.

———. *You Are What You Love: The Spiritual Power of Habit.* Grand Rapids: Brazos, 2016.

Smither, Edward L. *Augustine as Mentor: A Model for Preparing Spiritual Leaders.* Nashville: B&H, 2008.

Sorenson, Jacob. "The Summer Camp Experience and Faith Formation of Emerging Adults." *Journal of Youth Ministry* 13/1 (2014) 14–40.

Stanley, Paul D., and J. Robert Clinton. *Connecting: The Mentoring Relationships You Need to Succeed in Life.* Colorado Springs, CO: NavPress, 1992.

Stier, Greg. *Gospelize Your Youth Ministry.* Arvada, CO: D2S, 2015.

Stott, John, *The Message of 1 Timothy and Titus.* Downers Grove, IL: InterVarsity, 1996.

Stroope, Samuel. "Social Networks and Religion: The Role of Congregational Social Embeddedness in Religious Belief and Practice." *Sociology of Religion* 73/3 (2012) 273–98.

Struthers, William M. *Wired for Intimacy. How Pornography Hijacks the Male Brain.* Downers Grove, IL: InterVarsity, 2009.

Taylor, Edward W., et al. *The Handbook of Transformative Learning: Theory, Research, and Practice.* San Francisco: Jossey-Bass, 2012.

Thiselton, Anthony C. *1 Corinthians: A Shorter Exegetical and Pastoral Commentary.* Grand Rapids: Eerdmans, 2006.

Thompson, Augustine. *Francis of Assisi: A New Biography.* Cornell, NY: Cornell University Press, 2012.

Bibliography

Thompson, Graeme Campbell. "Keeping Close to Home: The Faith and Retention of Presbyterian Emerging Adults in Northern Ireland." PhD diss., King's College London, 2012.

Thompson, Judith, with Stephen Pattison and Ross Thompson. *SCM Studyguide to Theological Reflection.* London: SCM, 2008.

Torrance, James B. *Worship, Community, and the Triune God of Grace.* Carlisle: Paternoster, 1996.

Transparency International. "Nigeria's Corruption Challenge." May 2015. http://www.transparency.org/news/feature/nigerias_corruption_challenge.

Trinitapoli, Jenny, and Stephen Vaisey. "The Transformative Role of Religious Experience: The Case of Short-Term Missions." *Social Forces* 88/1 (2009) 121–46.

Turkle, Sherry. *Alone Together: Why We Expect More of Technology and Less from Each Other.* New York: Basic Books, 2011.

———. *Reclaiming Conversation: The Power of Talk in a Digital Age.* New York: Penguin, 2015.

Turner, Victor, and Edith Turner. *Image and Pilgrimage in Christian Culture.* New York: Columbia University Press, 1995.

United Methodist Church USA. "The Wesleyan Means of Grace." http://www.umc.org/how-we-serve/the-wesleyan-means-of-grace.

———. "Vital Congregations: Best Practices Report." 2012. http://www.umc.org/how-we-serve/vital-congregations-best-practices.

Vanhoozer, Kevin J. *Faith Speaking Understanding: Performing the Drama of Doctrine.* Louisville: Westminster John Knox, 2014.

Venable, Stephen F., and Donald M. Joy. *How to Use Camping Experiences in Religious Education.* Birmingham: Religious Education, 1998.

Voas, David. "The Rise and Fall of Fuzzy Fidelity in Europe." *European Sociological Review* 25/2 (2009) 155–68.

Voas, David, and Laura Watt. "The Church Growth Research Programme Report on Strands 1 and 2." February 2014. http://www.churchgrowthresearch.org.uk/UserFiles/File/Reports/Report_Strands_1_2_rev2.pdf.

Vrticka, Pascal. "Evolution of the 'Social Brain' in Humans: What Are the Benefits and Costs of Belonging to a Social Species?" *Huffington Post,* September 16, 2013. http://www.huffingtonpost.com/pascal-vrticka/human-social-development_b_3921942.html.

Walton, Roger. *Disciples Together: Discipleship, Formation and Small Groups.* London: SCM, 2014.

———. "Disciples Together: The Small Group as a Vehicle for Discipleship Formation." *Journal of Adult Theological Education* 8/2 (2011) 99–114.

———. *The Reflective Disciple: Learning to Live as Faithful Followers of Jesus in the Twenty-First Century.* London: Epworth, 2009.

Weale, Sally. "Teens' Night-Time Use of Social Media 'Risks Harming Mental Health.'" *The Guardian,* September 11, 2015. https://www.theguardian.com/society/2015/sep/11/teens-social-media-night-risk-harm-mental-health-research.

Wesley, John. "Sermon 2: The Almost Christian." http://wesley.nnu.edu/john-wesley/the-sermons-of-john-wesley-1872-edition/sermon-2-the-almost-christian.

———. "Sermon 16: The Means of Grace." http://wesley.nnu.edu/john-wesley/the-sermons-of-john-wesley-1872-edition/sermon-16-the-means-of-grace.

———. "Sermon 17: The Circumcision of the Heart." http://wesley.nnu.edu/john-wesley/the-sermons-of-john-wesley-1872-edition/sermon-17-the-circumcision-of-the-heart.

Bibliography

White, David F. *Practicing Discernment with Youth: A Transformative Ministry Approach.* Cleveland: Pilgrim, 2005.

Whitney, Donald S. *Spiritual Disciplines of the Christian Life.* Rev. ed. Colorado Springs, CO: NavPress, 2014.

Wilhoit, James C. *Spiritual Formation as If the Church Mattered: Growing in Christ through Community.* Grand Rapids: Baker Academic, 2008.

Wijnen, Harmen van, and Marcel Barnard. "Connected to the Wellspring: Ecclesiological Capabilities of Small Groups." *International Journal for the Christian Church* 13/3 (2013) 208–21.

Willard, Dallas. *The Great Omission: Reclaiming Jesus' Essential Teachings on Discipleship.* New York: HarperCollins, 2006.

———. *The Spirit of the Disciplines: Understanding How God Changes Lives.* New York: HarperCollins, 1988.

Williams, Brian A. *The Potter's Rib: Mentoring for Pastoral Formation.* Vancouver, BC: Regent College Publishing, 2005.

Witherington, Ben, III. *The Acts of the Apostles: A Socio-Rhetorical Commentary.* Grand Rapids: Eerdmans, 1998.

Withrow, Lisa R. "Disciples for the Future: Small Groups and Vital Faith Development." *Quarterly Review: A Journal of Theological Resources for Ministry* 23/2 (2003) 141–50.

World Council of Churches. "Together Towards Life: Mission and Evangelism in Changing Landscapes." 2012. http://www.oikoumene.org/en/resources/documents/commissions/mission-and-evangelism/together-towards-life-mission-and-evangelism-in-changing-landscapes.

Wright, Christopher J. H. *The Mission of God: Unlocking the Bible's Grand Narrative.* Downers Grove, IL: InterVarsity, 2006.

Wright, N. T. *Jesus and the Victory of God.* Christian Origins and the Question of God 2. London: SPCK, 1996.

———. *Surprised by Hope.* London: SPCK, 2007.

Wuthnow, Robert. *Sharing the Journey: Support Groups and America's New Quest for Community.* New York: The Free Press, 1994.

———. "Small Groups Forge New Notions of Community and the Sacred." *Christian Century,* December 8, 1993, 1236–40.

Wuthnow Robert, and Stephen Offutt. "Transnational Religious Connections." *Sociology of Religion* 69/2 (2008) 209–32.

Yaconelli, Mike. "The Failure of Youth Ministry." *Youth Worker,* June 2003.

Yust, Karen-Marie. "Creating an Idyllic World for Children's Spiritual Formation." *International Journal of Children's Spirituality* 11 (2006) 177–88.

Author Index

Laing, Mark, 95n7
Lanker, Jason, 59n4, 66n25, 67n28
Lawson, Michael S., 37n8, 38n10
Lenhart, Amanda, 121n1
Lewis, Bex, 124
Lewis, C. S., 49n5, 49n7, 51, 55n23, 56,
  57, 99n24
Lewis, Rick, 63n12
Lincoln, Sian, 12n2, 12n3
Linhart, Terry, 100n29
Livermore, David A., 101n43, 102n46,
  105
Lytch, Carol Eichling, xviin16, 28n16,
  41n22, 42n28, 43n31, 43n32,
  44n38, 89n30, 117n18

Mackenzie, Ed, 44n36, 46, 107n3
Mahan, Brian, 33n45
Mark, Olwyn, 40n19, 42n29
Martin, Todd F., 40n14
Martinson, Roland, 19n35, 28n21,
  114n12, 115n13
Mayo, Jeanne, xviin13, 57
McCabe, Scott, 90n34
McCarthy, David Matzko, 49n4, 117n20
McConnell, Scott, xvn5
McKnight, Scott, 27n15
Mezirow, Jack, 89n31
Middleton, J. Richard, 6n20
Miller, Patrick D., 38n11
Minear, Paul S., 26n7
Montgomery, Alice, 17n26
Murphy, Debra Dean, 32n40, 33n47

Nash, Sally, 29n23, 100n29
Newbigin, Lesslie, 93
Newby, Vicki, 92
Newport, Frank, 2n3
Nooney, Jennifer G., 17n24

Oden, Thomas C., 29n23, 106
Oestreicher, Jeannie, xviin12
Offutt, S., 103n50
Osiek, Carolyn, 74n14
Owen, John, 5n15

Packer, J. I., 33n47, 34
Parrett, Gary A., 33n47, 34
Parkinson, Cally, 19n34
Pattison, Stephen, 112n9
Pellitier, Joseph, 77n24
Peterson, Eugene H., 1, 11
Polycarp, 36n4
Powell, Kara, xviin18, 43n31, 67n26,
  94n6, 101n41, 103n47, 105, 119,
  124
Priest, Robert J., 99n27, 101n38, 103n51
Priest, Joseph Paul, 99n27, 101n38,
  103n51

Rainbow, Paul, 85n11
Rappaport, Roy, 31n33, 68n31
Regnerus, Mark D., xvii, 33n46
Reese, Randy D., 58, 59n3
Rhodes Jean E., 113n11
Richter, Phillip, 107n4
Ridley, Charles R., 70
Robbins, Mandy, 21n40, 29n24
Root, Andrew, xvn6, 2n5
Ross, Christine Lawton, xvin10, xviin19,
  32n38, 42n27, 55n25, 61n6,
  64n15, 65n22, 67n27, 79n37
Routledge, Robin, 3n10, 6
Runyon, Theodore, 107n2

Samuel, Alexandra, 122n3
Sandell, Jillian, 47n3
Sanders, Fred, 15n11, 16n15, 99n25
Savage, Sara, 21n39
Schnabel, Eckhard J., 97n18, 98n19
Schnase, Robert, 76n23
Schreiner, Thomas, 14n8
Schweitzer, Frank, 87n20
Segal, Alan F., 35n2
Sheer, Michael, 100n31
Shepherd, Nick, 53, 78n26, 79n32, 81
Sipe, Cynthia, 64n16
Smalley, Stephen S., 84n6
Smith, Christian, xiii, xvin11, 3, 8n28,
  17n23, 20n37, 21, 30n26, 31n31,
  32n41, 40, 41, 42n28, 44, 65n22,
  79n33, 99n28

Scripture Index

Joshua

6	38
7:1–26	14n7

Ruth

1	49n6

1 Samuel

3:1–9	61
18–20	49n6
18:1–2	49
20	49

2 Samuel

1:26	49
7:12–13	4

1 Kings

8:10	84
19:19–21	62

2 Kings

2	62
2:1	62

Nehemiah

8:1–2	14

Job

2:11	49n6
42:7–9	49n6

Psalms

1	50
1:1–2	9
33:20	37n6
38:11	49
41:9	49
78:4b	120
76:2	84
82:3	27
84	84
120–134	84
127:3–5	37
133	9
134:13–14	85
135:21	84

Proverbs

2:20	9
3:27–35	60
4	60
4:9	60
5:5–19	60
5:31	60
6:6–11	60
6:20–23	39
13:1	39
17:6	37
17:9	49
18:24	49
19:4	50
21:3	14
22:6	39
23:22–25	39
24:1	9
27:6	49
29:13	39

Isaiah

1:10–15	14
19:13	96
59:18—60:6	96

Lightning Source UK Ltd.
Milton Keynes UK
UKOW01f0625120617

303075UK00003B/409/P